CW00957690

GROUP WORK IN
EMBROIDERY

GROUP WORK IN
EMBROIDERY

BELINDA MONTAGU

B.T. Batsford Ltd · London

Drawings and photographs are by the author unless otherwise acknowledged.

ISBN 07134 4640 4

Typeset by
Servis Filmsetting Ltd, Manchester
and printed in Great Britain by
Anchor Brendon Ltd
Tiptree, Essex
for the publishers
B.T. Batsford Ltd
4 Fitzhardinge Street
London W1H 0AH

Contents

Acknowledgment

I would like to thank David Stagg, who so patiently deciphered my poor writing and typed the manuscript. I am also grateful for the willing assistance of my friends, and for the generous help and kindness given to me by many groups and individuals in my search for projects. I am especially grateful to Nancy Kimmins who provided photographs and advice. Constance Howard, Beryl Dean, Jane Lemon, Denise Bates, Kaffe Fassett, Molly Collins, Eddie Fenwick, Miss Bartlett and Canon the Rev. Peter Delaney kindly spent time answering my queries.

I would like to thank the following, who lent photographs: Elizabeth Ashurst; Cecil Higgins Art Gallery; Shelagh Dashfield; the Embroiderers' Guild; Diane Gelon; Maureen Helsdon; Susan Hill; Jane Lemon; Leila Riddell; the Royal School of Needlework; the Scottish Women's Rural Institute; Margaret Simpson; Muriel Tilling; the Toronto Guild of Stitchery; Gillian Watson. I am particularly grateful to Pat Grimshaw, who helped me with my photography.

I saw many wonderful projects whilst doing the research for this book; unfortunately, limited space forbids the inclusion of all of them.

BM
Kings Rew 1986

Introduction

'I think it as scandalous for a woman not to know how to use a needle as for a man not to know how to use a sword.' *Lady Mary Wortley Montagu*

The purpose of this book is to provide information and ideas for any group of embroiderers who are starting up and wish to organize and make a needlework project, however large or small.

Many groups are born out of a wish to commemorate in a tangible, visible and lasting manner the occurrence of some memorable event such as a royal visit, wedding or jubilee, the anniversary of a historical event such as the granting of a town charter, or even an invasion or battle. All these events can provide the necessary inspiration and opportunity for such an undertaking, and many projects of this nature are illustrated in this book.

There are many advantages to forming a group to work together. The group offers companionship, especially for people who do not go out to work and who are house-bound for most of the time; the work provides an opportunity to participate in something outside the domestic environment. Also, with leadership and encouragement, a group can share its knowledge, and help to develop individual skills; I have found that the more experienced and talented embroiderers are always extremely

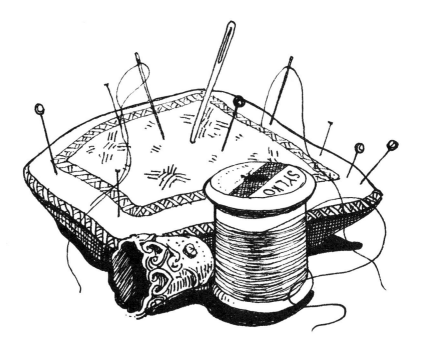

generous in passing on their knowledge and techniques. The individuals taking part will grow in confidence, improve their skills, make new friends, and experience the sense of community which comes from being part of a group involved in a worthwhile task.

The initial approach, planning and organization of a group embroidery project is of the utmost importance; questions about location and design, costing and finance and the formation of the group, perhaps from a nucleus of three or four experienced needlewomen, all have to be discussed in detail.

It takes a great deal of dedication, energy and enthusiasm to take a project through to completion, but the rewards of participating in the creation of a work which is of lasting value and much larger than could be accomplished by any individual working on her own, are many and wide-ranging. The end result can be a work of great merit, and something in which all the participants can take great pride.

The projects which I have included in this book range in concept, techniques and size from such ambitious works as 'The Dinner Party', created by Judy Chicago in America and symbolizing the history of women in Western civilization (a major part of this work being embroidery), to, at the other end of the scale, school projects; these are just as important because they encourage children to work creatively together and to take pride in their achievements.

In writing this book I have not attempted to deal in any great detail with the techniques employed, as there are many excellent books available which specialize in all aspects of embroidery. Instead, I have concentrated upon the experiences of the groups whose work is illustrated and described, upon the types of problems likely to be encountered and the ways in which these can be met, and upon the challenges and rewards of group work. From this, I hope that others may learn and benefit, and be encouraged should they wish to organize similar projects in their own communities.

1
Organization

Starting up a group

Initial organization is vital if a project is to be of the highest standard in every way, if the work is to run smoothly, and if everyone is to be happy. It is a great mistake to rush ahead to get started without first doing all the groundwork.

A small committee must be formed, including a leader or chairman; a treasurer; someone to look after the stock of fabrics and threads and allocate these to the workers; and someone to co-ordinate the research needed. There is much to be said for a small committee, but the number of members will obviously depend upon the size and complexity of the project and upon the number of workers involved, with further responsibilities being allocated as necessary and shared among the members of the group.

It is of great importance to avoid any clash of personalities, as this can ruin the happy atmosphere which must prevail. It should be a pleasure and a privilege to be part of a team, working to create something of lasting excellence.

Organization and the division of responsibilities are much easier when a project is undertaken by an existing group such as a Women's Institute or Embroiderers' Guild branch: the members already know one another, and are familiar with the skills and resources available within the group.

1 Members of the Romsey Quilters' Guild. (*Romsey Quilters' Guild*)

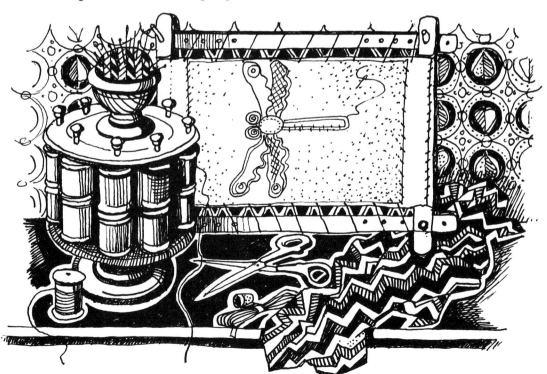

Leadership

The successful starting of a new group depends very much upon finding the right person to lead and organize. The group leader should have not only a knowledge of embroidery techniques and plenty of energy and enthusiasm, but also tact and experience in dealing with people. It will be necessary to teach and encourage those with less experience who may lack confidence in their ability, and perhaps also those who have previously only worked from kits and feel they might not be up to working alongside more experienced needlewomen. Everyone has to start somewhere, and most people have little idea of their capabilities until they become involved; as the project grows, so do their skills. The leader of a project has to encourage those who have ideas and wish to express them, while at the same time helping those who simply wish to carry out the work they have been allotted.

Costing

When endeavouring to estimate the cost of a piece of work, there are many items to take into account. You will have to assess the costs not only of the fabrics and threads, but also of overheads such as heating, lighting, telephone calls, stationery and postage, travel and petrol. In this day and age, it is not fair to expect people who give their time freely to a project also to be out of pocket, unless they wish to be generous in this respect.

With most group projects, no price is put upon the time given, the joint effort to create something of lasting value being both the objective and the reward in itself; but if a professional designer is employed, then a fee will be charged. Other costs which may need to be taken into account include those of making up or framing the completed work if this is to be done professionally, and of transporting it to the place where it is to be displayed.

It pays to use the best-quality materials for the work. If a great deal of time and effort is to go into a project, it is a false economy to use 'cheap' fabrics; though there are plenty of honest, plain fabrics which are not necessarily the most expensive and which may be just right for a particular job.

It is very important not to underestimate the expense of a project: try to anticipate all possible expenditure, so that enough money is available to complete the project without worry.

Fund-raising

Often it falls to the group to raise funds to finance the project. Coffee-mornings, jumble sales, and all the usual fund-raising activities are useful, but do also look to local commercial and industrial firms. They are often only too happy to be associated with a prestige enterprise connected with the arts, which will be good for their public relations. What may be a relatively small sum to a business can go a long way towards financing the work.

Also, I have found that some manufacturers, if approached, will be very generous with materials such as off-cuts of fabrics, leather scraps and so on. Laura Ashley actually recognize the demand, and sell packs of left-over pieces from their manufactured merchandise.

Research

Help from outside the group should be brought into researching the project, as this both helps to ensure accuracy and also broadens the community interest and involvement. Whether it is school children, a local historical society, or a natural-history group who are involved, the work will benefit from the help of people with a knowledge of the subject, who may provide information and ideas that might otherwise be overlooked. When using any heraldic devices, consult and have the design passed by the Royal College of Arms. It is very important that the authenticity of a project should not be spoiled by unnecessary mistakes.

Make scrapbooks, collecting illustrations from magazines, postcards and any material relevant to your project. This costs next to nothing and can provide a constant source of information.

2 The Silver Jubilee cope, a project conceived, designed and organized by Beryl Dean. Here J. Miskin, Beryl Dean and Sister Kathleen are applying the individually embroidered churches to the cream wool. (*Beryl Dean*)

2
Design

Planning the design and techniques

Whatever the project, whether it is work for the church or a decorative panel for a town hall, many of the same rules apply. The most important is that the design must be considered as a whole and in relation to the existing architecture and decoration of the building in which the work is to be displayed.

The basic idea, the most original and suitable way of conveying the visual message or story, often arises in group discussion. Someone hits upon an idea which seems exactly right. But how can you interpret the idea using symbolism, colour, line and texture? Should the design echo existing features, lead on the eye, or add

warmth to a dark corner? At what height will the design be viewed? Will there be daylight or artificial lighting? Should lighting be specially installed to illuminate the project? What is the best technique to employ, taking into account the scale of the project and the varying degrees of skill of the workers? Should it be worked in sections and then put together, much of the work being done in people's homes, or should it

3 The Maidenhead Charter hanging, designed by Jan Beaney and Jean Littlejohn. The embroidery is made up of three panels, each 213 × 122 cm (7 × 4 ft), and is worked in machine and hand embroidery. (*Dudley Moss*)

be worked on a large frame in a studio with several people coming to work together at a time? If so, where can a workroom be found with good light and heat in winter, which is accessible to all those taking part, and within reach of a good public-transport system and car park?

These are all considerations which need to be taken into account at the very start of the project. Usually, the concept of the design and the techniques to be employed are dictated by the site, which also fixes the dimensions of the work. These limitations and constraints help to resolve the difficult choices: it is always easier to work within specific requirements.

Employing a professional designer

If there is no experienced designer within the group, I recommend that a professional designer is employed, even if this necessitates raising extra funds.

For a large and important project a good design is essential. No matter how superbly the embroidery is carried out, if the design is poor then all is in vain. The Rev. Canon Peter Delaney, who designed the felt and hessian banners in Southwark Cathedral, said:

I think it important to underline the fact that though amateurs or semi-professionals might be encouraged actually to do the work, that is the appliqué, the laying down and the cutting-out, it is essential that the designing is done by professionally trained people. After all, a bad design leads to an unsatisfactory piece of work, however excellent the group working on it.

However, an artist or designer who is not familiar with embroidery techniques will need guidance from a skilled needlewoman who can visualize and translate the design into stitchery; ideally, the two should work together.

How to make your own designs

I think everyone should have a try at making his or her own designs, even if a professional is brought in for large projects. First, assemble all the information, such as the dimensions and notes from researchers, decide upon the possible techniques to be employed, and consider whether it is to be a purely decorative design or one that tells a narrative story (like, for

example, the Quaker project – page 38). Then start by making small sketches to explore ideas. Try to work on sheets of drawing-paper pinned or clipped on a drawing-board. I think this is less restrictive than working in a sketch-book – though it is invaluable to get into the habit of keeping and using a sketch-book to record ideas. Invest in some good-quality B and 2B pencils and a soft eraser, and keep your pencils sharpened.

Produce a large number of sketches, and do not be afraid to make notes upon them. Then take the best and most interesting features from your sketches, and from these work out your design. Make a paper shape the actual size of the work, and on this block in the larger shapes. These can be cut from coloured paper or thin card, and moved about until a pleasing arrangement is achieved. A putty-type adhesive is excellent for fixing a design temporarily until it becomes permanent and can be glued down. Pin up the designs and stand well back to consider the proportions.

Tracing-paper is very useful for working a design on, particularly for those who say they cannot draw. Trace, for example, the outline of a figure from a photograph, to give you a silhouette; by making several tracings you can repeat, reverse, and overlap the figures, moving them about until an interesting design is obtained. Cut and torn paper, as used by the children of Crestwood School to make their design (4, 5), is a good way of achieving a simple and bold effect. Simple shapes can always be made more interesting by using textured fabrics, or by varying the direction of the stitchery or quilting.

Try to look at the things around you with a fresh eye, as if you were seeing them for the first time. To draw something from memory, from your head, is difficult and the result is usually dull, but if you look closely at the real thing you will find that nature is far more inventive than the human imagination, so learn to look and question. Take two L-shaped pieces of card and put them together to make a window which is adjustable. Take, for example, a pot plant. Look at it through your window and adjust the frame until an interesting composition is found. Sometimes a small section will make a most exciting design which can be used in all kinds of different ways.

Always take your design, together with colour cards, swatches of fabrics and threads to experiment with, and look at them on the site where the work is to be displayed. Stand back and assess the strength of your design. A design which may look very bold on the drawing-board in your house may almost disappear when put in a setting where it has to be read at a distance.

Presenting your design

If, as usually happens, the designs have to be submitted to a committee who may not have much idea about embroidery, try to present them in a professional way.

Mount the sketches on card, making sure that they are neatly arranged and square with the edges of the card. Annotations should be typed or clearly written, and carefully positioned and mounted. Samples of fabrics and threads should be stapled or stuck in position to indicate the tone colours and textures. Make a small sampler to show the technique and stitches to be employed.

If you take trouble over the presentation, the committee or sponsors will be impressed, and will feel confident that the project is worthy of their support.

Transferring a design on to fabric

To those who have never transferred a design on to fabric, the prospect may seem daunting. There are several methods which can be used, but care must be taken to keep the design lively. Do not just trace the outlines without seeing the movement, and remember the techniques to be employed.

Pricking and pouncing
This is, perhaps, the most satisfactory way to transfer a design. Mark the centre of your tracing-paper by drawing lines down and across, line it up with the centre of your design, and draw around the outline. Then lay your tracing on a piece of folded felt, and prick with a needle around the outline, making perforations. When this has been done the tracing should be held up to the light to check that the design reads well.

The next stage is to line up the centre-marks

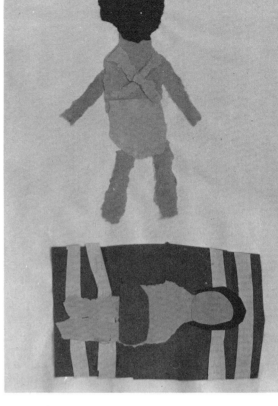

4 One of the many torn-paper designs representing summer, worked by the children of Crestwood School. The best features of many children's ideas were then put together to make an applied fabric hanging.

5 The next stage shows a cut-paper mock-up using a combination of torn-paper designs.

of the tracing on the fabric, and pin in position. Make sure that the fabric is lying firmly on a flat surface. If the fabric is on a frame, it is necessary to build up a flat surface underneath.

Pounce is a powder, either powdered charcoal or powdered cuttlefish, and is rubbed through the perforations using a pouncer made of felt rolled into a small pad. A circular, dabbing movement is used to work the powder through the holes, but care must be taken not to use too much as it tends to be messy and smudge. Shake the surfeit powder off the tracing.

Next the dots must be joined up to outline the design. A very fine brush is needed, and black, white, or grey water-colour paint can be used. If the embroidery is subsequently to be washed, or dampened to be stretched, water-colour (and

ball-point pen) will come through and stain the work; instead, a permanent medium must be used such as waterproof ink, oil paint thinned with turpentine (make sure the paint is completely dry before starting work), or acrylic paint which dries immediately.

Using a light-table
An easy method of transferring a design is to use a light-table. A home-made version can be improvised by placing a thick sheet of glass

A home-made light table.

between two chairs of the same height, or two tables. Put a lamp with a bright bulb underneath the glass, but not so close as to overheat the glass and possibly break it. Then place the design on the glass and the canvas on top, taping them both to the glass with masking or adhesive tape to prevent any movement. Measure both the design and the canvas to ensure that the design is centred on the canvas, and mark so that an even margin is achieved.

Other methods
Another method is to trace the design on to tissue paper, pin in place on the canvas, then tack around the outline. Afterwards the tissue paper is torn away.

Alternatively, the design motifs can be cut out from the paper, pinned in position on the canvas, and the outline drawn around. This cut-paper method gives you the freedom to design creatively, as the motifs can be moved around on the fabric until the desired effect is obtained.

An experienced designer can mark out a design straight on to the fabric using tailor's chalk.

Sometimes it will be convenient to photograph a large design, make up a slide, and project this on to the fabric which should be stretched on a frame. The outline can then be drawn around.

3
Panels and wall-hangings

From early times textiles have been decorated and embellished by needle and thread, whether by professionals or by amateur needlewomen at home, supplying the Church or royal patrons with wall-hangings, exquisite vestments and garments.

I think it likely that embroidery workshops were in being by the early tenth century; the stole and maniple of St Cuthbert found at Durham seem to have been produced by a group of embroiderers working together. It is sad that we know so little about those who worked in conditions that we would now think impossible. Very few pieces of their work remain, but one important embroidery which has miraculously survived is the Bayeux Tapestry. This is not a woven tapestry but an embroidered wall-hanging over 70 m (230 ft) long. It presents the story in pictures of the events leading up to the invasion of England by King William in AD 1066, including the crossing of the Channel, and the defeat and death of King Harold at the battle of Hastings. It was almost certainly commissioned by Bishop Odo of Bayeux, the half-brother of King William, and is thought to have been designed and embroidered in England by English craftswomen. It was not designed as a religious decoration to hang in a cathedral, but as a secular record of historical events. The eight strips of linen on which the design was drawn would have been stretched on frames to allow the team of embroiderers to work with both hands. This must be the earliest surviving example of a group project, although much of the information about its origins must be based on speculation.

We are indeed lucky in Britain to have a tradition of embroidery which goes back so far.

When I was commissioned to design the New Forest 900th Anniversary embroidery, I was able to turn to the Bayeux Tapestry to see King William, the founder of the New Forest, and to consider how he was represented by embroiderers in his own life-time. It was an extraordinarily close link over 900 years. When in 1965 Hastings was preparing to celebrate the 900th anniversary of the battle, it was suggested that the town should have its own embroidery, and both this and the Overlord Embroidery, which was made by the Royal School of Needlework to commemorate the D-Day invasion of France, owe something to the Bayeux Tapestry: they tell the story of the two most important cross-Channel invasions since the time of the Romans.

With the coming of the Tudor monarchs, life became more stable and settled. Fortified castles and keeps gave way to manor houses, and trade with the Far East expanded with the setting up in 1505 of an English Company of Merchant Adventurers; silk was one of the main imports. The aristocracy and the new wealthy mercantile class turned their attention to furnishing and decorating their new houses with wall-hangings and cushions.

In the Elizabethan period noblewomen would work together with the help of the household maids, the work often being directed by a professional embroiderer. Mary Queen of Scots was a skilled needlewoman, and during the long hours of her imprisonment in the custody of George Talbot, the sixth Earl of Shrewsbury, she worked with Talbot's wife Elizabeth (Bess of Hardwick) who was also an accomplished needlewoman. Together they planned and worked the embroideries and furnishings for Chatsworth, the house Bess was then rebuilding. The designs for many of the embroideries came from woodcuts and birds and beasts in books such as Conrad Gesner's *Icones animalium* and Claude Paradin's *Devises heroiques* as there were no ready-made designs in those days. Bess, the imprisoned Queen and her maids and ladies-in-waiting, would ply their needles as a group. Bess is known to have persuaded even the grooms and boys of the household to take part. Many of these embroideries can be seen at Hardwick Hall, which now belongs to the National Trust.

The Stoke Edith hangings, which are now to be seen at Montacute House in Somerset, are very fine examples of large, canvas-work wall-hangings dating from the early eighteenth century. They are so large that they must have been worked by a professional group, but it is not known where they were embroidered. The designs are typically English and were taken from prints of the period, but it has been suggested that they may have been worked in the Far East.

These early examples of the embroiderer's art should be studied for the information they provide on traditional techniques, many of which can be adapted and used to advantage in contemporary work.

In recent years there has been a revival of interest in wall-hangings and panels, and since the 1960s a number of important projects have been completed. Many were carried out by large groups under the guidance of experienced de-signers and embroiderers, but others were worked by smaller groups, not necessarily with professional assistance. The panels and hangings included in this book have been selected from the highly professional and from the more modest, many of which have achieved a very high standard. Architectural subjects lend themselves particularly well to being divided into individual sections for groups to work on, and many recent projects have been based on buildings of all kinds.

Greenwich Adult Education Institute's panel

This panel was designed by Mary Rhodes to celebrate the 50th anniversary of the Greenwich Institute, and was produced in 1963 by some of her students at the Institute.

The design shows an owl holding the torch of learning, and includes representations of drama, music, flower arrangement, pottery, art and the needlecrafts. The two coats of arms are those of Greenwich and the London County Council. The colouring of the background

6 The Greenwich Adult Education Institute panel (1963) designed by Mary Rhodes. The design shows an owl holding the torch of learning, and is worked in silk and vegetable-dyed wools. (*Mary Rhodes*)

changes from orange-rust for autumn, through to green for spring, to blue and yellow for the summer term. It is worked on 16-mesh canvas using silk and vegetable-dyed wools.

The panel can be seen at Charlton House, Charlton, London SE7.

The Hastings embroidery

In 1965, when Hastings was preparing to celebrate the 900th anniversary of the Battle of Hastings, the organizer of the celebrations, Group Captain Ralph Ward, suggested that Hastings should have an embroidery, a modern-day Bayeux Tapestry, which would be a pictorial history of Great Britain throughout the 900 years. The Royal School of Needlework was commissioned to undertake this vast and challenging project. The embroidery measures 74 m (243 ft) and consists of 27 panels each 274 cm (9 ft) long by 91 cm (3 ft) high, depicting 81 great events in British history.

The panels are worked by hand in appliqué in a wide variety of fabrics, with couched cords and threads used to define the figures and architectural features. The feathers used were

7 Group Captain Ralph Ward and Miss Allum (right) discussing work on the Hastings embroidery. (*The Royal School of Needlework*)

obtained from the bird-house at the London Zoo, the tweed from Scotland, and some fabrics from the Victoria and Albert Museum. The atmosphere of the embroidery reminds me of a glorious illustrated history book. The work took 22 ladies ten months to complete.

The St Clare panels

To commemorate the Diamond Jubilee of the Embroiderers' Guild in 1966, a panel was designed by Margaret Nicholson depicting St Clare of Assisi. She is believed to have been the patron saint of embroiderers.

The intention was that the design could be made into a transfer, both as a souvenir of the event, and also to be available to members as a basic design which could be adapted and used by those who were involved in church embroidery but lacked drawing skills. St Clare holds a monstrance, but this could be substituted by a lily for St Mary, a wheel for St Catherine, or a tower for St Barbara.

Eight members of the Guild volunteered to work the design, each in a different range of techniques and fabrics, and the resulting panels show how varied and personal the interpretations were. It is very interesting to see how the emphasis of the different features and areas can be changed by the imaginative use of techniques and stitches. The project shows how each individual, though working to the same design, can interpret the work through his or her own version to produce completely different results.

A rewarding and interesting project for any group would be to take a basic design, and let each person work in a different technique – patchwork, drawn fabric, blackwork, quilting, and so on.

Panels for Coombe Hospital, Kingston-on Thames, Surrey

Twenty-six 30 cm (12 in.) panels were embroidered with letters of the alphabet; each letter was then detached and mounted on hardboard. The panels were designed by Elizabeth Ashurst and made in 1974 for the children's ward of Coombe Hospital by the Textile Workshop, Kingston Adult Education Centre, during a six-week summer course.

21

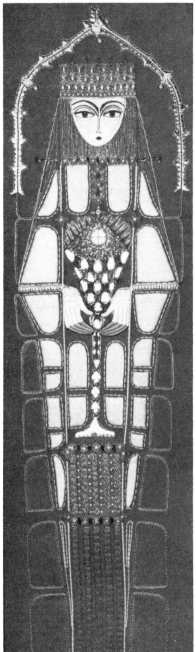

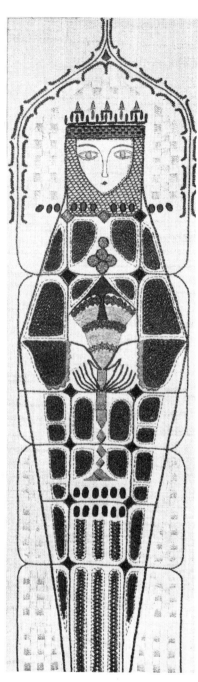

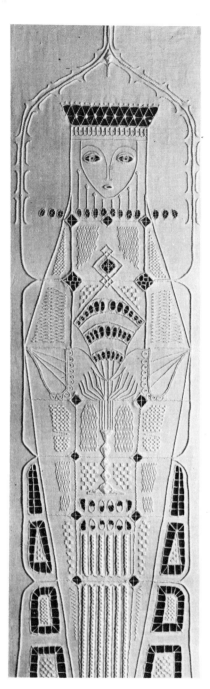

8 One of the eight panels of the St Clare embroidery, by Barbara Manning. The mosaic-like appearance was achieved by applying turquoise silk in many shades on khaki facecloth, with the edges turned in. The monstrance held in St Clare's hands is padded gold kid set with pearls. (*The Embroiderers' Guild*)

9 A St Clare panel by Susanna Pearson. Apricot-pink coarse woven silk fabric was chosen as a background for the many examples of filling stitches worked in a range of purple threads of different thicknesses. The dark and light tones of fig. 8 are reversed here. (*The Embroiderers' Guild*)

10 Here St Clare is interpreted by Mrs M. Crookes in cutwork, using fine white linen. The effect is both clean and delicate, and it is a good example of the use of a wide variety of stitches to fill in areas with interesting textures. (*The Embroiderers' Guild*)

22

11 Alphabet for Coombe Hospital, Kingston-on-Thames, designed by Elizabeth Ashurst. There are 26 30-cm (12-in.) panels embroidered with letters of the alphabet. (*Elizabeth Ashurst*)

The Greenwich Heritage panel

The original idea for working the Greenwich panel was put forward in 1974 by Mrs Maureen Bryant, one of the embroidery tutors at the Greenwich Adult Education Institute. The following year, 1975, had been designated International European Architecture Heritage Year, and Chester and Greenwich, as places of great architectural beauty, had been chosen to represent England's heritage.

The panel was designed by Mary Rhodes, a further-education tutor at Greenwich and Eltham Adult Education Institutes, and author of several books on embroidery. The panel, which depicts some of the fine buildings of the borough, was worked by students of embroidery at the two institutes.

The panel is mounted on calico, which was first washed and stretched upon a strong wooden stretcher. The size was large to work on – 244 × 122 cm (8 × 4 ft) – which made for problems only solved by working the panel in a vertical position with some workers at the front and others at the back, passing the needle to each other backwards and forwards at the exact spot required. At times as many as ten people were working in this way.

The background is in three shades of green velvet, divided into strips of varying widths and joined so that two narrow strips of the darkest tone encroach on to the medium tone, and the medium tone encroaches on to the light tone in the centre. By this method the change of tone does not appear too abrupt. The velvet background was stretched over the calico foundation, tacked all round, and 'squared-up' with cotton threads to enable the motifs to be correctly placed.

The expertise of the needlework tutor was sought in carrying out the somewhat tricky joining of the velvet strips, and the woodwork tutor provided the wooden stretcher and the finishing frame, thus involving other members of the institutes as well as those from the embroidery departments. Mrs Bryant's students were responsible for the lettering, and the embroidery of the buildings was divided between the students of Mrs Bryant and Mrs Rhodes.

The Heritage panel hangs in council chamber no. 4 of the Woolwich town hall, and can be viewed on request.

Depicted on the panel are: top (from left), Eltham Palace, the Greenwich coat of arms, the Royal Brass Foundry; centre, Woolwich town hall, Charlton House, the Queen's House, Plumstead House; bottom, the Royal Naval College, the *Cutty Sark*.

The Chester embroidery

To mark European Architectural Heritage Year in 1975, the Chester Arts and Recreation Trust initiated the idea of a large, canvas-work embroidery in which a number of people could participate; Diana Springall was commissioned to design the work. The entrance lobby of the town hall, though rather dark, was chosen as the most suitable site, as it offered a large wall space and the opportunity to incorporate four friezes, each 610×61 cm (20 ft $\times$ 2 ft), and a large main panel. Each frieze depicts a different theme in the history and development of the town.

The design is bold and simple, and the colours are restricted to five – pink, black, white, scarlet and brown. After much consideration, it was decided that these colours seemed to typify the essence of Chester. The main panel measures

12 The Greenwich Heritage panel, designed by Mary Rhodes, which commemorated International European Architecture Heritage Year (1975). The panel measures 244×122 cm (8 $\times$ 4 ft) and is worked in appliqué on a background of three shades of velvet. (*Mary Rhodes*)

13 The main panel of the Chester embroidery by Diana Springall, also designed to celebrate International Architecture Heritage Year. The design (610 × 228 cm – 20 ft × 7 ft 6 in.) is in pink, black, white, scarlet and brown canvas stitches; it represents the Spirit of Chester. (*Diana Springall*)

610 × 228 cm (20 ft × 7 ft 6 in.), and on it the shapes of the buildings, both ancient and contemporary, make for a bold and strong composition. The race-course and zoo are represented by, respectively, galloping horses and a family of elephants. The only human figures are those of the jockeys riding their horses to the finishing post. The countryside around the city is represented by a herd of black and white Friesian cows which produce the milk for the famous Cheshire cheese. Many of the embroiderers who worked the project came from rural areas.

Only two stitches were used: tent stitch, and, in contrast, velvet stitch, for which a dowel rod was used. These were chosen as suitable stitches for a project in which so many different needle-women of varying skills would be working side by side. Working frames were constructed of 5 × 2.5 cm (2 × 1 in.) soft wood, and on these the canvas was stapled, after the edges had been bound to prevent fraying. For the final mounting, stretchers of pine were obtained from C. Roberson & Co. Ltd, and before being stapled in position the embroideries were first stretched

on to damp blotting-paper and pinned down overnight.

The 71 metres of 101 cm (40 in.) wide canvas, German linen of 12 holes to 2.5 cm (1 in.), was purchased from Mace and Nairn of Salisbury. 84.5 kg (185 lb) of Wilton carpet wool were used at a cost of £443.93. The needles were donated by Milwards.

Three hundred women, aged from 11 to 85 years, took part; the enormous task of co-ordinating the work being undertaken by Mrs Katie Thompson, together with Diana Springall. Initially, classes and workshops were held to make sure that everyone knew the method and could achieve an acceptable standard of work. The panels were housed in various homes throughout the district while they were being worked, and many friendships were made through the project. The project led to the formation of the Chester branch of the Embroiderers' Guild, with Mrs Thompson as the first chairman.

This major creative work was achieved through joint sponsorship. The design fee was funded by the Crafts Council, and an exhibition of 'Work in Progress' and the permanent collection of the designs were sponsored by North West Arts. Chester District Council was responsible for the framing and mounting of the project in the town hall, and many local organizations and individuals held events to raise funds.

14 The Hounslow Civic Centre embroidery
(488 × 518 cm – 16 × 17 ft), designed by Barbara
Siedlecka. The hanging is in wools on canvas, with
carpet applied to give pile textures. (*Barbara
Siedlecka*)

The construction of the Hounslow Civic Centre
embroidery.

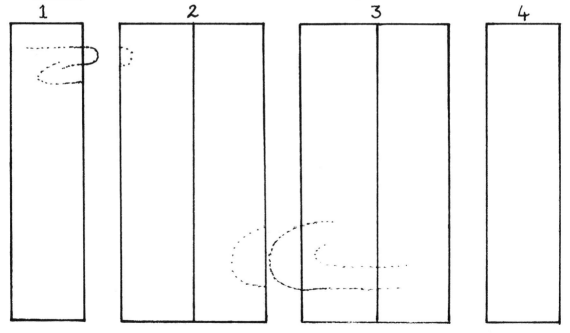

Hounslow Civic Centre embroidery

This large embroidery (518 × 305 cm – 17 × 10 ft), was designed by Barbara Siedlecka and worked with the help of Alison Barrell, Marjorie Self, Nancy Kimmins and Margaret Gaby of the Beckenham Textile Studio.

The Textile Studio at the Beckenham and Penge Adult Education Centre came into being in 1969 to enable advanced students of the embroidery department to work independently and experimentally, and to give them the opportunity of meeting like-minded people to exchange ideas, to teach, and to visit exhibitions. Barbara Siedlecka, who is primarily a designer and illustrator, did experimental work in the use of fabric, paint, wax and plaster to enrich the surface textures.

The Hounslow embroidery is worked on six widths of rug canvas. For working, the centre sections were joined so as to make four panels, the two outer ones being of single-canvas width, and the two inner ones of double-canvas width.

The design, which features the environment, was drawn on to the panels, but the choice of stitches was left to the individual workers; where a design ran into adjoining panels, the stitch would be decided by consultation.

The embroidery was worked using pieces of applied Wilton carpet, Wilton thrums, and many weights and combinations of wools, tufted and stitched in a variety of ways. The textures are rich and interesting and the colours subtle. When the four panels were finally joined, and the applied pieces of carpet overlapped, it was impossible to spot the joins. Applied carpet was used not only to save time, but also because it was intended that the hanging would be used to deaden sound between two public rooms. It was originally hung on a specially built-in rail, but has since been moved to another position.

Hanging for the Chailey Heritage Craft School for Physically Handicapped Children

In 1977, a wall hanging 244 × 91 cm (8 × 3 ft) was made over a period of about a term by the Kingston Adult Education Centre Workshop for the children's common-room of the Chailey Heritage Craft School.

The design was based on an imaginary street scene. Each student designed her own building, applied it separately to the hessian ground, and added surface stitchery and surrounding detail. The hanging is shown in colour plate 1.

The Thames Ditton and Weston Green wall-hanging

In 1977, as a result of seeing a magazine photograph of an American Bicentenary quilt, the idea was born that the ladies of Thames Ditton should do something similar to celebrate the Queen's Silver Jubilee.

Those involved were not particularly skilled embroiderers, and the project was planned in a spontaneous way to be finished in six weeks. The result is lively and represents a visual record of the village at that time. Already there have been changes – shops have gone or ownerships changed – and the wall-hanging is viewed with nostalgia by local residents, in the reading-room of the public library where it hangs.

The embroidery consists of 64 rectangles grouped into four panels, and worked in appliqué. They are mounted on Laura Ashley green sprigged cotton, and the predominant colours are the blues of the sky and the browns of the houses.

The whole has a naïve quality. Julia Hickman, Jane Formby, Marney Park and Rosalind Beavis organized the work, which proved to be an excellent community project, bringing together people who otherwise might never have met. It also served to inspire other work; the Worth Matravers Women's Institute started a similar project under the guidance of Julia Hickman's mother-in-law.

This project also featured on BBC TV's *Nationwide*, which must have been an exciting recognition for those who worked so hard.

The Bunyan embroidery

This embroidery was designed in 1977 by Edward Bawden to commemorate the Queen's Silver Jubilee. It depicts John Bunyan behind bars in prison awakening from his dream, the basis of the story of *Pilgrim's Progress*. The prison bars divide the 150 × 236 cm (5 ft × 7 ft 9 in) canvaswork panel into 80 squares; these were worked individually by the members of the needlework section of the Bedford Music and Arts Club.

The Thames Ditton wall-hanging.

15 The Bunyan embroidery (1977) designed by Edward Bawden RA. The panel (150 × 236 cm – 14 ft 11 in. × 7 ft 8 in.) is divided into 80 canvas-work squares. (*The Trustees, the Cecil Higgins Art Gallery, Bedford*)

Cross stitch was used throughout, except on the border, which is worked in long-armed cross stitch. Twenty shades of Appleton's crewel wool were used, predominantly in browns and greys, but with the celestial gate shining in bright golden yellow.

The embroidery can be seen at the Cecil Higgins Art Gallery, Bedford.

The Toronto historical embroidery

In the summer of 1977, two members of the Toronto Guild of Stitchery, May Horne and Ivy Clark, visited England and saw many embroideries, including the Hastings embroidery. Upon their return to Canada, they suggested that to commemorate the 150th anniversary of Toronto, their guild should embark on an embroidery based on its history, to be presented to the city. The idea was accepted by the Arts Advisory Committee of the city hall, and it was proposed that when completed the embroidery should be permanently displayed in the new city hall.

A study group was formed to carry out the historical research, and several artists were invited to submit designs. Finally, the general membership voted to accept a design by Barbara Gordon, who at that time was still a student at the Ontario College of Art.

The embroidery measures approximately 730 × 183 cm (24 × 6 ft) and is divided into three sections. The nine background panels show the

progress of the city's growth, from forest, water and sky, through the early settlement of York, to the present-day skyline of Toronto. This large area is hand- and machine-quilted using appliqué, embroidery and surface stitches. The forest is depicted by bands of leaves worked on a curve, based on the elliptical shape of the city hall. Among the buildings represented are settlers' cabins, Fort York, St Lawrence Market, the old city hall, apartment buildings and office towers.

The central section runs the full width of the background. On this narrow band progresses a cavalcade of 96 figures who have made Toronto what it is today, including the original inhabitants – the French and English settlers – the more recent immigrants, and individuals who have contributed to the history of the city.

The embroidery is framed at each end by canvas-stitched borders representing the city's coat of arms in a repeat pattern. The work took three years to complete with 140 guild members working on it. All their names are stitched on a piece of cloth enclosed between the embroidery and its backing. Also on the back are small pockets containing spare fabric and threads, in case any repairs are necessary in years to come. The total time spent on the work was 11,000 hours, but this does not include time spent on such things as planning, telephoning or typing.

The cost of the project was $14,000, half of which came from Wintario, and the rest from the guild. In total, 150 m (507 ft) of fabric were used, 29 different shades in the background alone, 443 spools and skeins of yarn, and thread in 159 colours. A great deal of work was done by individuals, but usually the stitchers worked in groups in the homes of 16 members, organized by 17 supervisors.

The embroidery can be seen in the city hall, Toronto.

16 The Toronto historical embroidery (1978) designed by Barbara Gordon. The nine panels show the growth from forest, water and sky to the present-day city of Toronto. (*Toronto Guild of Stitchery*)

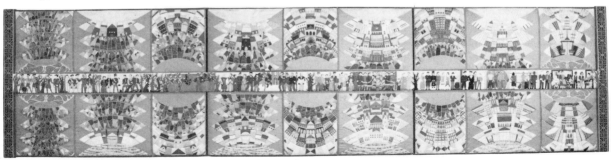

The Beaulieu Women's Institute village hanging

In 1978 a project with the theme of 'Our Village' was planned by the Women's Institute. Beaulieu decided to participate, and Sheila Belson undertook to design a fabric collage.

The village lends itself well to the making of an interesting panel. Palace House and the Gate House, which overlook the river, together with the church once formed part of the Cistercian monastery founded by King John in 1204. Village life still prevails in spite of the number of visitors welcomed in the summer. The village cricket team plays, children learn to sail their dinghies, and the seine-net is hauled in on the river bank. The mill, fire station, school, village hall, garage, garden centre and shops are all depicted on the embroidery; even the cormorant which is often to be seen perched on a post in the mill-pond, holding its wings to dry, is shown.

The project took one year to complete, eight members meeting at two-week intervals to work together. A talk on fabric collage was arranged at the start of the project.

The work can be seen in the village hall, Beaulieu, Hampshire.

17 The Beaulieu Women's Institute village hanging (1978) designed by Sheila Belson.

18 The friendship hanging, made by friends for Julia Walker, to decorate her new kitchen. (*David J. Walker*)

The friendship hanging

This hanging was made for Julia Walker by friends, each of whom contributed a square. The colours used were limited to red, green, black, grey and white. The designs were the choice and creation of the individual workers, and the final assembly was by Julia Walker. The hanging measures approximately 150 cm (5 ft) square and was made to brighten a dull kitchen in a new house. The work was completed in 1980.

The artists concerned were:

Mary Fogg	Renee Leale	Barbara Hanson and daughters	Susan Haddon (sister-in-law)	Jill Fitzpatrick
Irene Dobson	Nancy Kimmins	Valerie Riley	Pat Salt	Pat Wood
Rosemary Sabroe	Joan Cooper	Pam Warner	Tanya Walker	Margaret Gabbay
Louise Haddon (niece aged nine)	Janice Lawrence	Marjorie Self	Barbara Siedlecka	Victoria Haddon (niece aged six)
Cynthia Singer	Monica Perry	Pat Wood	Jean McGill	Dinah Travis

The Sleeping Beauty panels

The Sleeping Beauty panels were made to commemorate the royal wedding of Prince Charles and Lady Diana Spencer in 1981. The project was carried out by members of the Bishop's Stortford branch of the Embroiderers' Guild and the work took over five months; many of the embroiderers learnt the techniques as they applied them to the panels. The completed panels were presented to the St Elizabeth Home for Epileptics in Much Hadham, where they are greatly appreciated by the children.

The four panels, which tell the story of the fairy-tale, were designed by Sheila Pittock, an art teacher. The first panel depicts the christening of the princess, the second shows her pricking her finger, the third shows the castle with the prince striding in search of his princess through an enchanted landscape full of birds and animals; the final panel shows the bedchamber with the prince arriving to kiss the princess.

Some 60 embroiderers took part, and many different techniques, threads and fabrics were used. Cards of the embroideries were produced for sale in aid of the Home.

19 A panel from the Sleeping Beauty embroidery, designed by Sheila Pittock and made by Bishop's Stortford Embroiderers' Guild for a children's home. (*Bishop's Stortford Embroiderers' Guild*)

20 The Sleeping Beauty embroidery: the princess pricks her finger. (*Bishop's Stortford Embroiderers' Guild*)

21 The castle in the enchanted landscape, with the prince in search of the princess. (*Bishop's Stortford Embroiderers' Guild*)

22 The arrival of the prince. (*Bishop's Stortford Embroiderers' Guild*)

The Maidenhead Charter hanging

The Maidenhead Charter hanging was commissioned by the mayor of Maidenhead to mark the 400th anniversary of the granting of the town's charter. It was designed by Jan Beaney and Jean Littlejohn, and its bold and simple design greatly enhances the rather stark interior of the town hall where it hangs.

The three panels each measure 213 × 122 cm (7 ft × 4 ft) and were worked by 70 embroiderers, members of the Windsor and Maidenhead branch of the Embroiderers' Guild and of the embroidery department of Windsor and Maidenhead College; several men were among the needleworkers. They worked a total of 2,250 hours over a period of 20 weeks.

The hanging combines machine and hand embroidery. The flowers in the foreground are in brilliant puces and pinks, the centres worked freely in machine embroidery; in contrast, the three roundabouts and the bridges are hand-quilted. The trees, grass and leafy areas are hand-stitched in a variety of threads.

The panels portray the essential features of the town: the two important Thames bridges, the river and the flora of the parks and gardens.

23 A detail of the Maidenhead Charter hanging, designed by Jan Beaney and Jean Littlejohn. (*Dudley Moss*)

The Newcastle 900 Anniversary panel

The following account of how the Newcastle project was approached, researched in depth and carried out, was supplied by Mrs L.A. Davis. It is a most helpful record and should be of interest to any group embarking on a similar project.

'In 1975 the Newcastle branch of the Embroiderers' Guild was asked by several councillors if it would be willing to take part in the city's 900th anniversary celebrations. This was agreed, subject to a satisfactory project being found, and to the branch not being involved in heavy expenditure. Subsequent meetings took place at which various ideas were put forward by councillors and members of the Guild.

'A subcommittee of four Guild members was appointed to consider the various ideas, and it was finally agreed to make an embroidered panel of historical interest, but until we knew where it was to be placed, the size and cost could not be worked out. After many more meetings and consultations it was agreed that the panel would be hung on a large wall of Westmoreland Seate, on the second floor overlooking the main staircase of the Civic Centre. The size – 505 × 183 cm (16 ft 7 in. × 6 ft) rather overwhelmed us, but by this time members of various committees, including librarians, architects and antiquarians, became very interested and offered to help us compile our subject matter, which we realized must be complete and correct in every detail. The Guild subcommittee, consisting of chairman, treasurer, artistic adviser and co-ordinator, had decided that the

24 The Newcastle 900 Anniversary panel (505 × 183 cm – 16 ft 7 in. × 6 ft), worked by the Newcastle branch of the Embroiderers' Guild. (*City of Newcastle upon Tyne, City Engineer's Photographic Section*)

panel should display events of historical importance to the city from the year AD 43 to 1983; and as the city owed much of its wealth and success to the river, the various panels would be built up around it.

'Before stitching could commence, many months of research went into the many subjects suggested. Finally it was decided to embroider 24 panels, 14 approximately 46 × 35 cm (18 × 14 in.) and ten 46 × 76 cm (18 × 30 in.); these were to surround five large centre panels. The next items to be decided were colours and materials, bearing in mind the restrictions imposed by the vivid red carpets in the Civic

Centre. It was finally agreed to use grey dupion for the background (this was obtained from France); the surrounding panels were to be in various blues and greens to denote the river; the three main panels were to be red, with two intermediate panels of grey. The material we chose for the coloured panels was Sapphire Cascade, the embroidery cottons DMC.

'The designs for the panels were gradually built up with help from the City Library and Art Galleries. Several very artistic Guild members then proceeded to draw these out, ready to be transferred to the various panels. Meanwhile members produced samples of their work, and were selected to embroider the panels. Our working headquarters was in an old library, and here members were instructed by the four members of the subcommittee as to what was required of them. Each working member was handed a pack containing design, material,

35

threads and suggestions for stitches and colours. From time to time the workers were brought in for further guidance.

'To the relief of the committee, two members offered to work the two large red panels, one depicting the city's churches, the other famous buildings in the city – a colossal task. The centre panel and focal point, showing eight special buildings and events in the history of the city, were to be worked by skilled embroideresses in gold and metal threads. The two large grey panels, showing the industrial development of the city through the ages, were to be worked in machine embroidery. The five panels were to be united at the base by the "History of the Town Moor".

'In the meanwhile the five giant frames were being constructed by a city craftsman, all to be finally bolted together to hold the completed panel. Each frame on completion was carefully covered with strips of domette which were glued on, the corners being skilfully mitred and stitched. When quite dry, dupion was stretched and laced at the back using waxed fishing line. This lacing was pulled taut at regular intervals for a fortnight to ensure that no creases or folds appeared.

'Gradually the whole scheme began to take shape, but not without many anxious moments, such as when the mice from a nearby churchyard decided to invade the library during our absence and make some very cosy nests in the domette at the corners of the frames!

'It was a red letter day when the first panel was completed; at last the project was beginning to take shape. As yet, we had not decided how to attach the panels to the frame. Many methods were tried and finally it was decided to mount the panels individually on card, and use cord round the edge.

'About this time the civic committee suggested that a sponsor be found to cover the whole cost of material, frames, and mounting. To our satisfaction, Rington's Tea Company agreed to donate a substantial sum. To show our appreciation, a small replica of the famous Rington's tea van was included on the machine-embroidered panel.

'The day arrived when we could no longer work at the library, so our precious panels were transported to the Civic Centre in five large vans supplied by Rington's. We worked with the frames on huge trestles, gradually building up our masterpiece. Each panel was attached to the appropriate frame using surgical needles. This was done by only a few skilled needlewomen. During this time, the "History of the Town Moor" was steadily being stitched, and many members who had not previously been able to help enjoyed sharing in this section. Indeed, on one group of trees no fewer than 11 members took part.

'The day came for the panels to be bolted together – a very tricky task undertaken without mishap. It was estimated that the five panels together weighed over 1,000 kg (1 ton). It now remained for the three centre panels to be attached, which proved a very tedious task. All the panels were finally joined together, and the next step was to fix the embroidery on the slate wall. Special brackets had been prepared to receive it, and it took 18 men (including our sponsor and the Lord Mayor's secretary) to lift it into position. Finally, a silver cord was sewn all round it. Our task was completed, and it was ready to be handed over to the city by the sponsor's wife on St George's Day.

'In all, 57 of our Guild members took an active part in the task. These included not only the embroiderers, but others who assisted in many of the unseen tasks connected with such an undertaking. It proved an excellent opportunity to get to know not only our members, but also their families who assisted in many ways.

'The panel took two years of hard work and research. The estimated cost of the whole project was £5,000, including materials, frames, mounting and glazing. We spent nine months on the stitching, and we used: 33 m (108 ft) of grey dupion, 18 m (60 ft) of Red Cascade, 11.5 m (37 ft) of various blue and green fabrics, 50 m (164 ft) of white linen for backing and frames, 23 m (75 ft) of domette, 159 m (587 ft) of thick and thin cords, 2,352 stranded cottons, 63 reels of sewing thread, 42 packets of needles, waxed fishing line for lacing the frames, ten large tubes of glue and three large cops of twine.'

The Croydon Centenary panel

This 305 × 183 cm (10 ft × 6 ft) panel was designed by Moyra McNeill and worked by members of the Croydon branch of the Embroi-

25 The Croydon Centenary panel (1984) designed by Moyra McNeill. The panel measures 305 × 183 cm (10 × 6 ft) and is worked in appliqué, patchwork, canvas stitches, and machine and hand embroidery. (*The Advertiser, South Croydon*)

derers' Guild. It was presented by the Guild to Croydon Corporation to mark the centenary of the borough's charter in 1984.

The design incorporates all aspects of Croydon life – civic, commercial, industrial and recreational – as well as houses and landmarks, both past and present. Fifty members of the Guild worked on individual pieces, which when completed were mounted on to the background fabric. A variety of materials was used, including silk, cotton, canvas, wool, nylon, ribbon, velvet and acetate. The techniques employed include appliqué, patchwork, canvas work, machine and hand embroidery.

The panel hangs in the entrance to the town hall, mounted under glass, and is best viewed from the first floor.

The Overlord embroidery

The Overlord embroidery is another project undertaken by the Royal School of Needlework, although it is very different in feeling and design from the Hastings embroidery (page 21). It tells the story of 'Operation Overlord', the code name for the Allied invasion of Normandy in June 1944. This work was commissioned by Lord Dulverton, who himself served in Normandy in 1944, as a memorial to the men of the Allied Forces, and to the civilians in industry, agriculture, civil defence and the merchant navy who made possible the defeat of the German armies in France.

The embroidery consists of 34 panels each

26 Members of the Royal School of Needlework working on the Overlord embroidery, supervised by Miss Bartlett. (*The Royal School of Needlework*)

244 cm (8 ft) long and 91 cm (3 ft) high, and measures 83 m (272 ft) in length. It was designed by Sandra Lawrence under the supervision of a committee of senior officers representing each of the armed services. She was also advised by service historians in the Ministry of Defence. In the workrooms of the Royal School, 20 embroiderers worked for five years to complete the panels, accurately reproducing Sandra Lawrence's design, and applying many different fabrics including original battledress khaki and gold braid to give authenticity to the panels. It is now in its permanent home in the Southsea Museum, Portsmouth, and is most beautifully illuminated and displayed. It is not only an example of outstanding craftsmanship, but also a moving historical record.

The Pebble Mill Heritage tapestry

Kaffe Fassett, who is well known for his beautiful knitwear and canvas-work designs, was always fascinated by the sixteenth-century Oxburgh hangings embroidered by Mary Queen of Scots and Bess of Hardwick. These provided him with the inspiration for a very popular group project of phenomenal size. As Kaffe wanted as many people as possible to participate, he approached the BBC programme *Pebble Mill at One*. He appeared on the programme in 1984 to launch the idea, asking viewers to embroider a 15 cm (6 in.) canvas-work square; the theme was to be 'Count Your Blessings'. Sponsorship and promotion of the idea was undertaken by the Wool Marketing Board and Liberty's of London.

Over 2,500 squares were sent in; even the male programme-presenters contributed squares! These were sorted into boxes by subjects – dogs, cats, houses, birds, beasts, churches, sports, flowers, gardens, landscapes, etc. Twelve squares featured Jane Torvill and Christopher Dean who at the time were enchanting us all with their brilliance. Before the squares could be put together and mounted, borders had to be stitched round each square. This huge task, together with the sewing together of the squares, was undertaken with the help of many art students from all over the country. Julia Lewandawskyi, together with members of the Kingston branch of the Embroiderers' Guild, assembled 14 panels made of 784 squares, working in the exhibition room of the Guild's headquarters at Hampton Court. These panels will eventually be on display at Chatsworth House, Derbyshire. The remaining squares have been made into hangings for Pebble Mill studios and also for the Wool Marketing Board; other panels are still to be made which will cheer up a children's home or a hospital.

Kaffe gave his enthusiasm, energy and precious time to this enormous project; he also provided the opportunity for a great many people to feel pride that they had contributed a small part of themselves by demonstrating gratitude for their blessings.

The Quaker tapestry

The idea of creating an embroidered history of

27 Kaffe Fassett in his studio, arranging the 2,500 squares sent in for the Pebble Mill tapestry.

the Religious Society of Friends (Quakers) first occurred to Anne Wynn-Wilson in 1981 as a co-operative activity for small and scattered children's meetings, and to provide opportunities for education, communication and group activity. When the 70 panels (each measuring 61 × 56 cm – 24 × 22 in.) are completed, they will display narrative designs depicting the story of Quakerism, honouring the spiritual insight, devotion and achievements of many Friends during the past three centuries.

Since 1981 the idea has grown into a large-scale project, involving workshops and residential courses spread all over the UK, and the formation of a supporters' group. The aims of the group are:

1 To spread information about the tapestry among Friends.

2 To encourage groups (including children) to – (a) Undertake research into the historical material on which designs could be based (and, originally, to suggest subjects for panels); (b) Accept a panel for embroidery and arrange for instruction in the skills required.

3 To organize fund-raising to support the tapestry financially.

4 To arrange exhibitions of the tapestry in meeting houses and elsewhere.

Members receive a newsletter twice a year, giving information about progress and details of workshops. The supporters' group numbers about 300, and many other Friends contribute to the embroidery.

A stitch, aptly named the Quaker stitch, was specially created for the lettering on the panels. This can be enlarged and built up by using four

In the tapestry panel:

1818-43 ELIZABETH FRY visited every ship taking women convicts·children to Botany Bay

106 ships, 12,000 souls

Women used to be taken to the docks in irons in open carts·This was ended·Many people helped to improve shipboard conditions

School·sewing groups were started for those who wished

Each woman was given a bag of useful things

28 A panel from the Quaker tapestry designed by Jo McCrum, incorporating children's designs in the lower section; embroidered by Anne Wynne-Wilson, Ann Castle and Australian embroiderers. (*Religious Society of Friends*)

threads of Appleton's crewel wool, and then forms a corded stitch which is suitable for the core of the large letters.

Interest has been worldwide, and in 1984 a prepared panel depicting Elizabeth Fry was taken on its frame by Ann Castle to Australia, where she gave talks and held workshops in Perth, Adelaide, Melbourne and Sydney; the panel was completed by Australian embroiderers, including children. It is hoped that the project will be completed by 1990.

4
The New Forest embroidery

The New Forest embroidery was commissioned by the New Forest Association to commemorate the 900th anniversary of the founding of the forest by King William. The New Forest Association is a charitable organization formed in 1867 to protect and preserve the unique character of the New Forest area. Finance for the project was given by local industrial organizations.

I was invited to design and organize the project, and thought that it would both speed up the work and add another dimension if local embroiderers were involved. Letters were put in local newspapers inviting 'experienced embroiderers' to volunteer their skills, and about 60 enthusiastic people, including two men, came

29 A detail from the first panel of the New Forest embroidery, showing the applied pieces of canvas work, each worked by a different embroiderer.

forward. All those who helped gave freely their precious time and skills.

An early step was to decide upon a suitable place where the finished embroidery could eventually be housed and displayed. After much consideration, it was thought that the Verderers' Hall in the Queen's House at Lyndhurst would be suitable for the purpose, and the embroidery was designed in three panels to be placed between the windows of the Hall; because the light was from the north, no direct sunlight would fall on the embroideries. It was not then known that the Queen's House was shortly to undergo major restoration, and that when this was finally completed the Forestry Commission for security reasons would be unable to allow pub   access to the Verderers' Hall to view the work. However, in the meantime the embroidery had already been completed and put on temporary display in the council chamber of the New Forest District Council at Appletree Court, Lyndhurst. The dimensions of the individual panels, together totalling 762 cm (25 ft) in length by 62 cm (just over 2 ft) in depth, now appear haphazard as they are not displayed in the setting intended; but it is hoped this will one day be rectified when a permanent home is found for the embroidery.

In planning the techniques to be used, I looked at other large embroideries, in particular at the Bayeux Tapestry in which King William, the founder of the New Forest, features many times. In researching the project, the help of the Nature Conservancy Council was enlisted to supply a list of the flora and fauna, and local historians were able to find more than sufficient material to fill the panels.

The embroidery was to depict 900 years of the life of the forest, the major historical events unfolding throughout its length. It was intended that the centre of each panel would be occupied by forest trees, with the seasons changing as time progressed. Along the top, in the foliage of the trees, would be heraldic devices associated with the events depicted below, and in the foreground would be the flora and fauna of the forest.

First I made small sketches which I submitted to the sponsors, together with a mock-up section showing the technique of applying canvas work mixed with other fabrics, with machine-work and hand-stitching used side by side. It is impossible to describe how the finished work will look to people who have no experience or understanding of creative embroidery, so it was important to prepare a mock-up. Also, it was very useful to experiment with the fabrics so that techniques could be evolved at the same time as the design, before work had advanced too far for changes to be made.

Next, I made a full-size cartoon upon which I pinned notes of how to work the sections, and samples of the fabrics and threads that were to be used. In order to achieve continuity, I had decided that I would work all the figures myself. The birds, animals, tree trunks, and heraldic shields were all to be worked by the helpers, some of whom lived at a considerable distance. The various motifs were traced and numbered on the cartoon, and records were kept of the number of the piece, the name of the worker, and the date when it was given out. When there are a lot of similar pieces they must be numbered, as it is very easy to get into a muddle. A kit was sent by post to each helper to work at home. I painted the design in acrylic paint on pieces of canvas, some of which had 16 and some 18 threads to 2.5 cm (1 in.), selected the Appleton crewel wools, and wrote instructions. All of this was most time-consuming, but on the whole it worked well.

Three wooden frames were constructed on which the sections of the finished embroidery would be stretched. Trestles, the height of which could be varied as required, were made to hold the frames when working. As I was using a great deal of machine embroidery and it was frequently necessary to take the work off the frame, I devised a method of attaching the work with bulldog clips; this allowed it to be pulled taut on the frame, but at the same time it remained easy to remove or replace. Bulldog clips are also useful for clipping material to the edge of the work-table when machining large sections which are heavy, difficult to handle and liable to fall to the floor.

The background, which was made up mainly of silks, taffetas and silk organzas, was applied first. This was followed by the tree trunks, the foliage overlapping the trunks, and the flora and fauna built up in the foreground. I had encouraged the workers of the tree trunks to use various stitches to add texture, particularly on oak trees which have rough bark.

As the completed pieces were returned, I cut them out, leaving a 6–12 mm ($\frac{1}{4}$–$\frac{1}{2}$ in.) margin of unworked canvas to be folded under and carefully stitched down to the back. With the smaller, intricate birds and animals this took quite a bit of manipulation, but it made it easier to apply them and kept their shapes crisp and neat.

I was worried that the panels might look 'bitty' as a result of using such a mixture of techniques, and having so many people working small pieces; however, I think the colour range of greens, soft browns and golds, successfully united the various elements. It is hard to find fabrics in the colours you need, especially when you live a long way from good shops, so I dyed different fabrics in batches of colours using Dylon hot-water dyes; by this method I was able to get a range of tones in the colours needed.

Two of the panels were finished in April 1979 for Her Majesty the Queen to see when she visited the forest for the 900th anniversary celebrations. In the subsequent third panel, I was able to include the Queen planting a tree on this occasion; she was dressed in a brilliant mustard-coloured coat and hat, decorated at the back with a bunch of blue ribbons, which I tried to match exactly.

Sadly, as my workroom is small (being the end of my bedroom), it was not possible for the helpers to meet to work together and see each other's progress, but some did visit me from time to time to see how the assembled work was progressing. Wherever possible, I think that much is to be gained by the workers on a project getting together for a few hours each week. We all learn from each other and discussion stimulates ideas.

The embroidery has become a valuable fundraising asset for the New Forest Association. A booklet, *The New Forest Embroidery*, describing and illustrating the events and features depicted, has provided a useful source of income to help the NFA to continue its efforts to conserve and protect the forest.

For myself, the opportunity of making the New Forest embroidery was a great pleasure and privilege, and a challenge which extended and stretched my techniques in needlework. It also broadened my appreciation and knowl-

edge of the forest, an area where I have ridden and hunted all my life, and which I love greatly.

The New Forest cushion

When Her Majesty the Queen visited the New Forest on the occasion of the 900th anniversary celebrations, she was presented with a cushion as a gift from the people of the forest.

The front, which depicts the flora and fauna of the forest surrounding the Rufus Stirrup, was worked by Mrs Midge Burnett. The back was worked by Mr Wilfred Aikman, a keen gardener and Saints (Southampton Football Club) supporter. On first meeting him one would never have guessed him to be an ardent, self-taught needleworker; he claimed that he learnt to use needle and thread as a Jackaroo in the Australian outback, where he had to sew on buttons and mend his own clothes. The cushion was designed by the author.

30 The cushion presented to HM the Queen by the people of the New Forest. Designed by the author

31 The cipher on the back of the New Forest cushion, worked by Wilfred Aikman.

5
Church vestments

Designing for vestments

The designing and making of church vestments must be of the highest possible artistic and technical standard; any group embarking on such a project will need expert advice and leadership from someone experienced in work of this nature.

When searching for a theme or message upon which to base the design, look at the unique architectural features, or the stained-glass windows, of the church where the vestments are to be used, and prepare sketches from these. Another possibility is to use a short text. Lettering can be an excellent source for design, but again the designer needs to have some basic knowledge of the principles of letter design. Find out the shape preferred for the vestment, and look at any other furnishings and vestments with which it will be used. Take colour-cards and samples of fabrics when meeting to discuss the project, and look at these *in situ*.

When presenting the design, mount the sketches on card, staple on samples of suggested fabrics and threads, and try to make a professional-looking presentation (see page 16). Provide a sample of the technique planned as this will enable someone not familiar with contemporary embroidery, and perhaps with not too good an imagination, to grasp and visualize what you have in mind.

Many people seem to have a fear of modern design, and consultations and discussions with the priest or vicar must be sympathetically and tactfully handled; gentle persuasion may be needed for a new approach to be accepted. The Church of England has in each diocese a committee of professional and lay advisers to comment upon designs.

At the start it is vital to discuss all the financial arrangements, and to determine how much money is available so that the project can

be properly costed. Within a limited budget, it may be necessary for Thai silks to give way to less expensive furnishing fabrics.

The organization of a church project is much the same as for any other needlework project, but the design and execution of the embroidery, and the making up, need to be very expertly done. Not only will there be more wear and tear than in the case of a panel made up as a wall-hanging, but the vestment will be expected to have a long life and not fall apart; this must be a consideration when planning the type of embroidery to be used and its placement on the vestment.

Liturgical colours

White and gold are generally used for All Saints' Day, Christmas, Epiphany, Easter, Ascension, Trinity Sunday, the Feast of Our Lady, baptisms, confirmations and weddings.

Red is used for the feasts of the Martyrs, Whitsun or Pentecost, the feasts of the Apostles and Holy Innocents' Day.

Yellow is used in the Church of England for the Feast of the Confessors.

Green is used for Epiphany, and the season from Trinity to Advent, and for everyday wear.

Blue and violet is used during Advent and for the first four weeks in Lent, for Vigils, Rogation Days and Ember Days.

Black is for funerals, All Souls' Day, and, in the Roman Catholic Church, for Good Friday.

Unbleached linen is sometimes used throughout Lent.

The chasuble

The chasuble is the correct vesture for the celebration of Holy Communion and is made in liturgical colours as part of the set of Eucharist vestments. This comprises the stole, maniple, burse and veil, as well as the chasuble. Over the centuries the shape of the chasuble has been modified and changed, and the one now most generally used is the Gothic Revival shape.

The embroidery for the chasuble can have equal interest on the front and on the back, and offers a great opportunity for a strong, simple design which will read well at a distance. This must be considered in conjunction with the design of the Eucharist set as a whole; if symbols are chosen to convey a visual message, these can

be used in different ways or in a reduced scale on the burse, veil and stole.

The fabric chosen for the chasuble must not be too heavy, but it should be of a weight that hangs well, does not crease, can be cleaned, and will be hard-wearing. Hand-woven silks 150 cm (60 in.) wide are made for the purpose and can be used unlined, but fine wools, cotton mixtures, and dupion are all satisfactory. When making a set in the same fabric, be sure that the grain of the fabric runs the same way on the chasuble, stole, burse and veil.

Once the design is decided upon, make a paper pattern and draw on the design, or cut it out in shapes of coloured paper or card and stick them on the pattern. The texture can be indicated with crayon or paint. Always look at your design, together with fabric samples, *in situ* in both daylight and artificial light.

Before cutting out the fabric, it is advisable to make a toile which can be fitted and any necessary adjustments made. Also press the fabric before cutting out. In cutting out, pin the pattern to the fabric and work on a flat surface; remember to leave adequate seam allowance.

You are now ready to transfer the design for the embroidery on to the fabric and frame up. Only the area to be embroidered needs to be stretched, so to protect and keep clean the rest of the fabric, roll it round a cardboard tube, or wrap it in tissue paper and tack around the edge of the frame (72).

The backing for the embroidery may be calico or cambric, and this should be washed and cut to the size of the area to be embroidered. This is matched in position with the centre of the design, pinned and tacked; try to keep the tensions of the two fabrics the same. The work can then be stitched into the frame and the frame tightened.

To make it possible for several people to work on a vestment, smaller areas of embroidery can be worked on separate frames and subsequently assembled and applied. There is, of course, no need to frame up if machine embroidery is to be used.

To make up a chasuble
Pin the pattern on to the fabric. When using 163 cm (64 in.) fabric the centre lines are placed to the fold of the fabric. Cut out carefully. Stitch the shoulder seams. Turn up 2–3 cm ($\frac{3}{4}$–1 in.)

The construction of a chasuble.

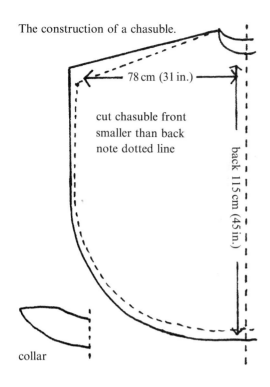

← 78 cm (31 in.) →

cut chasuble front
smaller than back
note dotted line

back 115 cm (45 in.)

collar

hems front and back. Pin, tack and press, where necessary making nicks in seams and removing wedge-shaped pieces.

For a lined chasuble, the linings should be attached to the front and back separately before being joined together. Place the lining, folded in half, down the centre line on the wrong side of the vestment, and with tie-tack stitches lock the centre of the lining to the centre front and back of the chasuble. When this has been done, unfold the lining and complete the zigzag tacking around the edge to hold chasuble and lining together. Next, turn in the lining around the hem line and slip-stitch through the fold of the hem, stopping about 8 cm (3 in.) from the shoulder line.

When this has been completed for the front and back of the vestment, the chasuble shoulders may be stitched together, making sure that the neck points match. Press these seams flat. The back lining is now caught down on to the chasuble seam turnings. The front lining can be turned under to the shoulder line, and slip-stitched into position on the back lining.

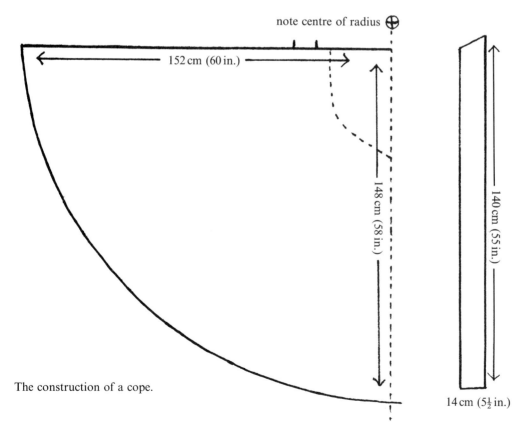

note centre of radius ⊕

← 152 cm (60 in.) →

148 cm (58 in.)

140 cm (55 in.)

The construction of a cope.

14 cm (5½ in.)

If a collar is not to be used, either a facing or piping is needed around the neck to make a neat and strong finish. The lining is then hemmed into position. Detailed instructions on the making of vestments are given in Beryl Dean's *Church Embroidery* and *Embroidery in Religion and Ceremonial*.

The Lenten vestments, Salisbury Cathedral

The pure-wool, hand-woven vestments were designed to complement the altar frontal, and to build up the image of the Cross.

The chasuble depicts the shadow of the Cross

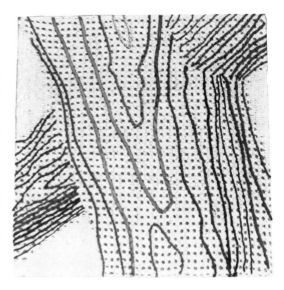

32 The chasuble for the Lenten set for Salisbury Cathedral, designed by Jane Lemon and made in pure wool by the Sarum Group. The chasuble depicts the shadow of the Cross thrown across the celebrant.

33 The burse for the Lenten set, showing the same design of the Cross as in fig. 32.

34 The stole for the Lenten set.

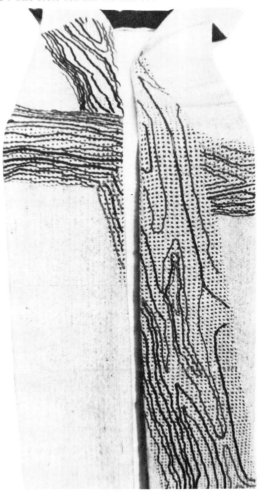

thrown across the back, almost as if the celebrant were carrying it himself. It is worked in drawn-thread work, with the grained effect of the wood inspired by the pronounced grain of olive wood. The stole and the burse are decorated with small areas of the same Cross.

The stole

The stole is made in two parts joined at the neck; each part is usually 137 cm (54 in.) in length, between 5 and 6 cm (2 and 2½ in.) in width at the neck, increasing in width to between 7.5 and 9 cm (3 and 3½ in.) at the two ends.

The embroidery can be of any suitable style, but frequently consists of a design based on the Cross, a small one at the back of the neck, and a larger design at each of the two ends. If the stole is to form part of a set, then the design will be taken as part of an overall plan. Fringes are now no longer used on stoles.

Draw out the pattern, and cut out the pieces with the grain of the material running lengthways. Frame up the backing and mount the two ends to be embroidered, rolling up the other ends and pinning them out of the way.

When the embroidery has been completed, remove from the frame and cut away the backing. Then join the centre-back seam, which should be slightly sloping. Cut two pieces of interlining a fraction smaller to fit inside, but overlap by 6 cm (2½ in.) at the centre back. Zigzag-tack at the join, and turn the interlining to the shape of the neck. Fold over the turnings on to the interlining, catch-stitch down, and press on wrong side.

Cut out the lining, allowing for turnings. Stitch the centre seam at the same angle as on the stole, press and open out. Match up the back seams, and place the lining in position, working outwards from the centre back. Pin-tack down the middle to keep in place, then, starting from the centre back, fold the lining under and slip-stitch.

The maniple is no longer used in modern services, but it is made up in much the same way as the stole. Instructions for the burse and veil are given in Chapter 6, Church Furnishings.

The cope

The cope is basically a semi-circular cloak fastened across the chest by the morse, which can be made of fabric or metal. It is worn usually by archbishops, bishops and deacons on ceremonial occasions. The band or border which runs along the straight edge is called the orphrey, and is usually approximately 10 cm (4 in.) wide, but it is not obligatory and whether or not it is required depends upon the design. In some copes the shoulders are fitted, which makes them more comfortable to wear.

The design should be dramatic as the cope, or copes when a set has been commissioned, are usually viewed at a distance. It can be an all-over design, as on Beryl Dean's Silver Jubilee cope, worked in 1977 by members of her class, or the embroidery can be confined to the hood and orphreys, as on the set of purple copes designed by Jane Lemon for Salisbury Cathedral (see colour plate 4). If the cope is to be without a hood, a large-scale design covering the back can be very effective, as this is the side frequently seen facing the congregation.

The fabric chosen should hang well and not crease easily, but it should not be too heavy. Fine wool, crêpe, dupion, velvet and Thai silk are all suitable fabrics. Very shiny and slippery linings should be avoided.

Work out the design on paper, taking into account the height of the incumbent who will be wearing it, then make a toile which can be fitted on the wearer. The usual length down the centre back is 152 cm (60 in.), and a simple way to make a pattern is to draw a semi-circle of the radius required. For this, a pencil can be attached to a piece of string of a length equal to the required radius, the other end of the string being pinned to the centre of the edge of the paper.

When cutting-out, be sure to leave enough material for turning up the hem. This should be pinned up during fitting, and the position of the morse indicated. Before completing the hem, allow the fabric to drop, otherwise the hem will be very uneven.

The embroidery should be worked on a frame, in a similar manner to that described for the chasuble, and the garment pieces assembled when the embroidery is completed.

The cope is made up in a similar way to the chasuble. Turn in the edges and hems, and lightly catch-stitch the lining in place on the centre back and seams, as described for the

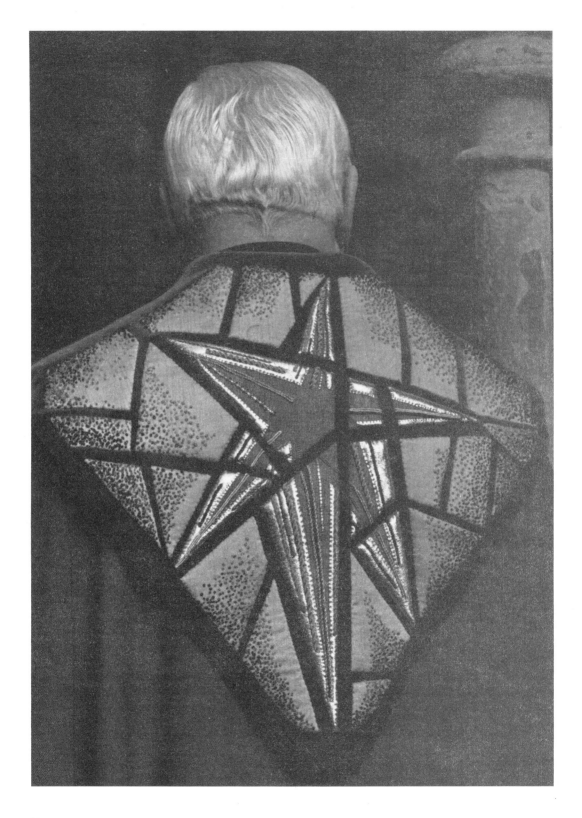

35 The hood of the precentor's cope of Salisbury Cathedral. The cope has a star motif representing the vision that claimed the Prisoners of Conscience.

chasuble. Make the morse and attach it and the hooks to a strip of material about 4 cm (1½ in.) wide, interlined with tailor's canvas or buckram; stitch it to the cope with strong button thread.

The making up of a cope or chasuble is not as simple as it may look at first, and the most splendid embroidery will be wasted if the vestment does not hang well in deep folds. Try to find someone with dressmaking experience to undertake the making up.

The Silver Jubilee cope

The Silver Jubilee cope was designed by Beryl Dean and worked by members of her class for ecclesiastical embroidery at the Stanhope Adult Education Institute, London. Four and a half months of intensive work produced a design

36 The Silver Jubilee cope (1977), a project designed and directed by Beryl Dean and carried out by her students at Stanhope Adult Education Institute, London, for the see of London. (*Millar and Harris Ltd*)

planned so that each unit could be worked separately; in November 1975 this was shown to the Bishop of London and his acceptance was obtained. The cope is unusual and exciting in design, with all the churches of London adorning it. The buildings are embroidered with gold and silks upon backgrounds of grey, fawn, honey colour and ivory-white organza, and applied to a cream-wool background. It is usually on show in the Treasury of St Paul's Cathedral, London.

Winchester Cathedral copes

Five festival copes were designed by Barbara Siedlecka and made by Nancy Kimmins, Moyra McNeill and students of the Beckenham Adult Education Centre, for the 900th anniversary of Winchester Cathedral. The designs were submitted to the dean in 1977, followed by life-size samples the following spring.

The four canons' copes are plain and mainly red when turned towards the congregation, but change to a rich texture and colour when viewed from the back. The panels of velvet are graduated in colour from deep crimson through scarlet, cinnamon and orange, to gold, divided by gold fillets. The hoods are individual in design and are based on the cathedral's roof structure; they are made in a mosaic of padded silks with gold interlacing. (See colour plate 5.)

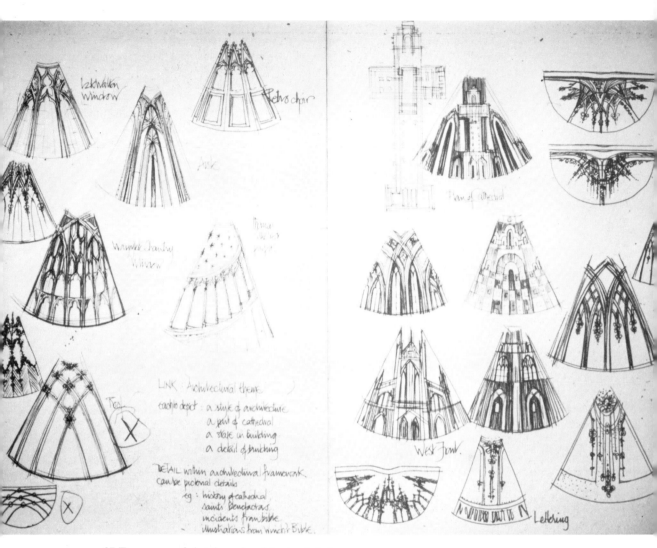

37 Two pages of sketches of architectural designs
for the Winchester Cathedral copes, by Barbara
Siedlecka. (*Nancy Kimmins*)

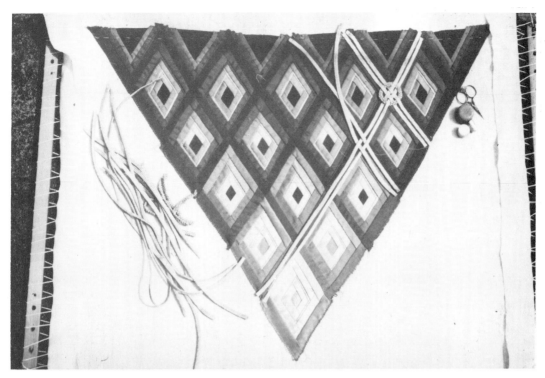

38 The hood of a cope for Winchester Cathedral: first stage. (*Nancy Kimmins*)

39 The hood being finished off by hand. (*Nancy Kimmins*)

6
Church furnishings

Altar frontals

The most important focal point in the church is the altar, the Lord's table. For a free-standing altar, a throw-over or Laudian is the simplest form of altar frontal. The dimensions depend on the height and length of the table, but the cloth should touch the floor all round. The embroidery for the cloth should not be too heavy, otherwise it will not hang well.

The problems of design and the means of fixing or mounting are different for every altar, as there is no uniform size or method of suspending the frontal, but if the embroidery is to be fairly heavy, the best results will be achieved by stretching the frontal on a frame. This means that it is kept taut, and does not have to be folded when not in use. The cover for the top and sides is made separately.

Patchwork is an excellent technique for working an altar frontal, especially for a group of mixed ability. Good examples of patchwork altar frontals are at Tetbury and in St Mungo's Shrine, Glasgow Cathedral. The Tetbury frontal is mounted on a frame and the sides sweep down and drape on the floor, creating a pleasing and lyrical shape which is echoed in the arrangement of the patchwork gradation of

Mounting up an altar frontal.

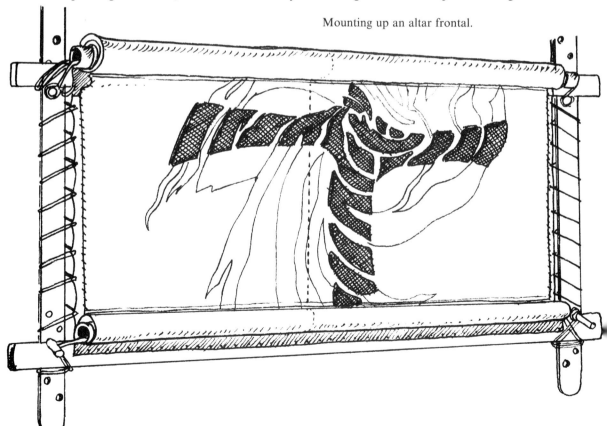

40 The Lenten altar frontal for the high altar, Salisbury Cathedral, designed by Jane Lemon and worked by the Sarum Group. The frontal shows the Prisoners of Conscience in pulled and drawn-thread work. (*Jane Lemon*)

colour and tone. If the design had relied just on the rectangle without the sides, the effect would have been very dull (for further details, see pages 57–8). At St Mungo's Shrine, Glasgow, is a patchwork Laudian altar frontal. This was designed by Malcolm Lochhead and worked by members of the Glasgow and West of Scotland branch of the Embroiderers' Guild.

Lenten frontal for the high altar, Salisbury Cathedral

The Lenten frontal for the high altar was designed by Jane Lemon, and worked by her and members of the Sarum Group. The frontal shows the congregation as rock-like figures upon whom the church is built. It is seen in unison with, and links with, the east window of the cathedral, which is dedicated to the Prisoners of Conscience. The figures are raised and padded, and are worked in pulled and drawn-thread work on a variety of linens, hessians,

scrims and open-work fabrics. The threads vary in weight from coton perlé no.12 to velvet ribbon and leather thongs.

The Sarum Group was formed in October 1978 from members of an embroidery class taught by Jane Lemon. An exhibition of the Group's works had been held in the cathedral, and the ensuing interest led to commissions from the dean and chapter, including two other large frontals for the high altar. These and many other commissions have kept the Group fully occupied.

The frontal for the Chapel of St Laurence, Salisbury Cathedral

This altar frontal was also designed by Jane Lemon. The altar top is the oldest in the cathedral, so the design needed to be strong; it was also important for the colours to complement those of the adjoining Chapel of St Margaret.

St Laurence was burnt to death on a gridiron in the third century AD. For the background a slubbed furnishing fabric of pale green was chosen. Zigzag rectangular patchwork across the bottom and up the sides represents the embers of the fire, while the flames lick upwards

41 The altar frontal for the Chapel of St Laurence, Salisbury Cathedral, designed by Jane Lemon and made by the Sarum Group. The frontal shows the gridiron on which St Laurence was burnt to death; the embers are in patchwork and the flames were applied separately. (*Jane Lemon*)

42 The burse for the St Laurence Chapel.

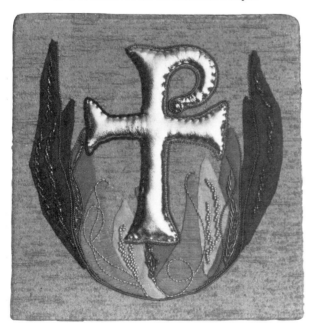

through a wrought-iron gridiron which was made in the cathedral workshops. Each of the flames was made separately in different fabrics, some shiny and others matt; they are in reds, pinks, oranges and yellows. The fabric was applied to pelmet vilene, and some pieces were strengthened with millinery wire, and highlighted with pearls, beads and metal threads in gold and copper.

The patchwork, made by Molly Lance, was applied to the background, which was stretched over a wooden frontal frame. The flames were applied, and the gridiron was screwed to a wooden batten at the back of the frame. Some of the flames were then curled through the gridiron. The flames and the assembly were made by Eddie Fenwick and Jane Lemon.

The cushion is worked in a similar zigzag rectangular patchwork by Eleanor Fielden. The stole and burse, which complete the set, were also made by Jane Lemon.

The Tetbury parish church altar frontal
In 1969 the Tetbury church needleworkers started upon a project to refurbish their church; a group of seven embarked upon the renewal of the altar-rail kneelers, using a design adapted by Sheila Yates from an Embroiderers' Guild design. They also worked some kneelers for the choir.

56

43 The stole for the St Laurence Chapel.

In 1981 the church celebrated a bicentenary, and to commemorate this the group decided to do some more needlework. The vicar, Michael Sherwood, suggested that a new altar frontal was badly needed to replace a red frontal which was very worn.

Jane Lemon was approached to make the designs, and she decided that a hexagon patchwork would be the most suitable, as this technique could easily be divided up for a number of people to work on at the same time.

The project was advertised in a local building-society window, showing photographs of the church, the designs and some samples of patchwork. Money was raised from coffee mornings, and Jane Lemon gave a fund-raising talk.

The designs were prepared by Jane Lemon as a full-scale mock-up, with the templates marked in with a felt-tip pen. In colour the frontal changed from a dusky rose-pink at the top to deep plum at the bottom. The fabric used was Parker Knoll furnishing fabric, and it took four months to cut out and tack the hexagons which were stitched with Coats Drima thread. Each

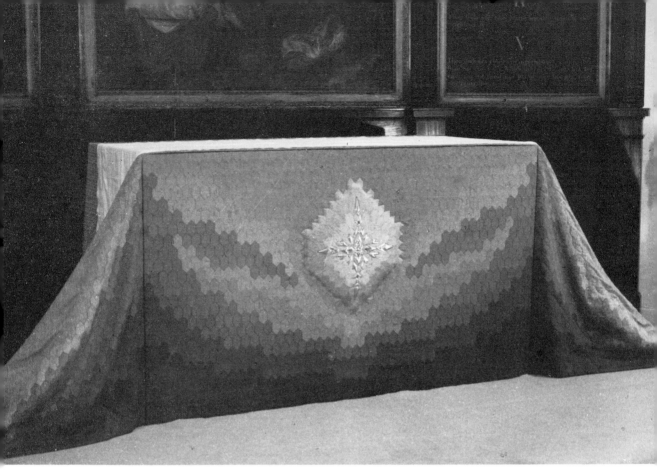

44 The Tetbury church altar frontal designed by Jane Lemon, made in patchwork in shades of pink.

embroiderer was given a numbered colour-chart for reference.

When the patchwork was completed, the tacking and paper were taken out, and the work was backed with calico and stretched on a frame. Self-fastening tape was upholstered along the top of the frontal and down the two sides of the frame, and stitched around the three sides of the altar cover (see diagram) so that the side pieces flow out from the frontal as if it were all one.

At the same time a cope, stole, burse and veil, cushion and pulpit fall were embarked upon. The two chairs which stand either side of the altar were given new canvas-work backs and seats, also worked from an adapted Embroiderers' Guild design.

The completed refurbishment is now unified in colour, and the subtle shades of rose-pinks are a perfect complement to the fine painting over the altar which is the focus of the eye when one enters the church. Rose-pink is not a colour often used, but it is quite acceptable as a general ferial colour to be used after Trinity.

The burse and veil

The burse and chalice veil are no longer statutory in the modern service, but are still used in some churches which follow the traditional service.

The burse, in which is kept the corporal, can be quite richly embroidered. The usual size is 23 cm (9 in.) square, it is hinged at the top, and stands hinged-side uppermost on the altar. The veil should not be too thick or have too much heavy decoration, otherwise it will not fold or hang well. The ornamentation should be in the centre of the front. The veil is usually 50–75 cm (20–30 in.) square, but the measurements depend on the size of the chalice.

To make up a burse
Cut two squares of side 23 cm (9 in.) from

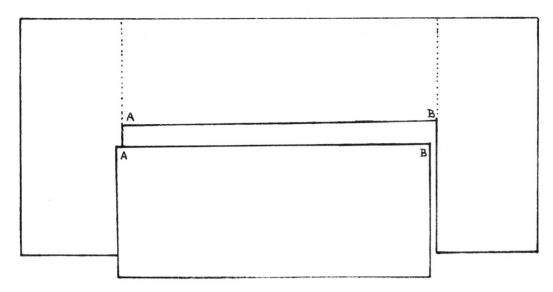

The pattern for the Tetbury altar frontal.

The construction of a burse.

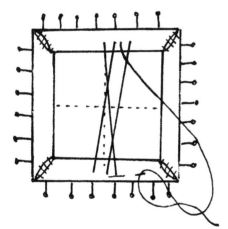

heavy-gauge box-card, and two from lighter card for the lining. Across the heavy card, mark the centres each way in order to position the design, which should be correspondingly marked with tacking stitches.

Place the embroidered front on the heavy card and pin in position around the edges. Lace across the back using strong thread, mitring the corners. I would not advise the use of glue as this makes it difficult to stretch the fabric really taut, and once set the pieces cannot be moved if

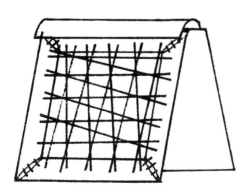

incorrectly positioned. Do not cut away the backing from the embroidery, as this acts as an interlining.

Similarly, place the back on heavy-gauge card, pin and lace. At the top, leave a wide turning to form the hinge. Next the two linings are placed on the lighter cards and pinned and laced, mitring the corners.

Place the front board back to back with a lining board and pin together, but leave the top open for the subsequent insertion of the hinge. Pin together the back board and the other lining board. The hinge strip, backed with a strip of lining, is now slipped between the front board and its lining. Fold the front and back boards together to check the positioning and make sure that they fold flat; then pin the hinge strip in position. Finally, ladder stitch all round, joining the linings to front and back.

Pulpit falls

The pulpit fall can be a focal point and provides a good opportunity to introduce colour and interest in the form of a design that complements the other furnishings. It is usual to follow the liturgical colour for the season for which the fall is to be used.

The size and proportions depend on the width of the lectern or stand, and almost any material can be used, provided that it is not too thick. There are two distinct ways in which the fall can be made. If the embroidery is heavy and three-dimensional, it should be stretched over box-card using the same method as that described for making up the burse, the top and front being made in one piece. Alternatively, it can be made in two pieces, the fall in the form of a banner sandwiched between two cards which rest upon the desk.

Making up the pulpit fall
For the first method, cut two pieces of box-card for the top and the fall, and two similar, lighter cards for the linings. If the backing of the embroidery has not been retained, interline with calico.

Place the embroidery face down, with the interlining tacked in place. Position the two thick cards on the fabric, leaving a narrow gap for the hinge; pin the cards in position and lace across the backs of the cards.

The construction of a pulpit fall.

Similarly, the lining should be backed with the thin boards and laced; if you are using thin silk it may be easier to fix in position with freezer tape instead of lacing.

Place the front and the lining together back to back, pin in position, and ladder stitch around the four sides.

For the second method, cut an interlining of heavy vilene or canvas. Place this on the back of the embroidery, turn in and catch-stitch down on three sides, leaving the top flat.

Line the back, attaching the lining on three sides with slip stitch, but again leaving the top, which is to be slipped between the two cards. The cards should be covered with the same fabric and lining.

Insert the front between two boards and pin together. It is usual also to secure a piece of elastic between the two boards and running

60

across the back; this helps to keep the pulpit fall in position on the lectern.

The two boards are then stitched together with ladder stitch around the sides and top, the fall being slip-stitched invisibly to the boards as illustrated.

Alms bags

The making of alms bags is a perfect small project for a church group and should be approached in much the same way as a kneeler project (see Chapter 7).

Alms bags need to be strong as they will have to stand up to a lot of wear and tear. If they are small, those who are taking the collection tend to roll them up and stuff them in their pockets, so try to avoid this by making them just too large for the pocket!

Canvas work is very suitable, because it is both durable and attractive. The bags may be either flat in shape, or attached to a mount. If you are making a pattern for a flat bag, cut the pocket piece wider across the mouth than the backing piece, or alternatively insert a gusset. The pocket lining should be of chamois or supercham.

45 An alms bag for Salisbury Cathedral, designed by Jane Lemon and made by the Sarum Group.

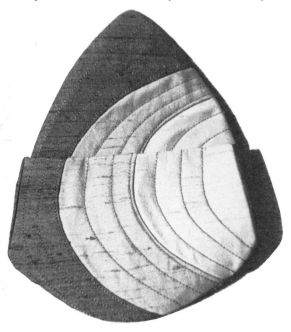

Church curtains and wall-hangings

Many draughty churches cry out for a heavy curtain to shut off a door or the vestry. To be effective, and also so that they will hang better, curtains should be interlined when they are made up, although this may not be necessary if the fabric is very heavy. The best embroidery techniques to use are appliqué and patchwork, both of which are very effective.

Wall-hangings lend themselves particularly well to very modern churches where there are large expanses of plain wall. A hanging can bring life and focus to an austere building. As a group project a hanging can also serve to unite the members of the parish, bringing people together to get to know one another better.

Romsey Abbey curtains

These curtains were designed by Maureen Helsdon, and worked by both full- and part-time students of embroidery at Southampton College of Arts. They were consecrated in 1966.

Two curtains, 4 × 2.3 m (13 ft × 7 ft 5 in.), are hung to fill a Norman arch in Romsey Abbey. The dark violet background sets off the saints with their traditional symbols. They are worked in appliqué with machine and hand embroidery.

The curtains at St Mary's, Nantwich

These curtains were commissioned in 1975 to hang over the west door of St Mary's church, to commemorate the Queen's Silver Jubilee.

The designs, which take into account the golds and reds in the stained glass and the warm red sandstone of the walls, were worked by Denise Bates, who is a talented painter. Full-scale drawings were prepared, then a toile was made, and much experimental work followed. Eileen Caswell took on the task of translating the design into embroidery, and of guiding the 20 ladies of the parish who joined together in 1981 to start work in the Bromley Chapel.

The theme of the curtains is 'Christ the Light of the World', and the text 'He that followeth me shall not walk in darkness, but shall have the Light of Life' is worked on the pelmet above the curtains. The first curtain depicts Christ in history, the Nativity, the shepherds, and the kings in Light. Above the Virgin is a canopy based on the tower of St Mary's. The second curtain features Christ in Glory, and the people

The Nantwich curtain being made in the church.

46 The Romsey Abbey curtains designed by Maureen Helsdon and worked by students at Southampton College of Arts. (*Maureen Helsdon*)

of today, from many nations, walking in the Light of Life. Above the Christ is a canopy based on the choir stalls, and below is the royal cypher and the date of the Silver Jubilee. The figures, heads and hands are worked in suede with sepia thread 'drawing' to link up with the figures in the windows above. The deep gold material for the curtains was a gift from Mr R.S. France of Haighton and Son Ltd. Each of the curtains measures 5×5 m (16 ft 4 in. square).

The group of ladies at Nantwich work with great enthusiasm and fellowship to beautify to the Glory of God their fine church, which is a familiar and cherished landmark. When they first embarked on the project many of them were inexperienced and lacked confidence, but this is now far from the case, and the standard of their work has advanced enormously. They have also worked a great number of kneelers. Those in the nave have various themes including the timbered houses so unique to the area, making a set which is simple and very successful; others show scenes from nature. The kneelers in the choir stalls depict early musical instruments. (See colour plates 6 and 7.)

Hangings at St Alban's Abbey
The group which made the four hangings in St Alban's Abbey was formed in 1972. They not only did general repair work, which at first took up much of their time, but also made stoles and other vestments, some of which were for other churches and individuals connected with the abbey.

In 1977 Gillian Watson was asked by the dean to reorganize the embroidery work, and to undertake the making of the four panels which now hang in the abbey. These were designed by Sister Regina of Cockfosters, and represent the Four Elements in Salvation: Water, Earth, Fire, and Wind and Spirit (see colour plate 10). They measure 305×122 cm (10×4 ft) and are mainly worked by hand. The frames upon which these large panels were worked were improvised from scaffolding poles wrapped in foam; these were

63

47 A detail of the curtains in Nantwich church showing the Nativity, designed by Denise Bates.

heavy and once set up could not easily be moved.

The width of the panels meant that it was impossible to reach the middle, so one person sat underneath to receive the needle and passed it back to the person on top. This was a very uncomfortable and laborious way to work, but the fact that the embroidery was stretched on scaffolding poles meant that it could not be rolled on a wooden embroidery frame.

Except in school-holiday time, the group still works every Thursday morning in the north transept of the abbey. This is not ideal as it is cold in winter, lighting is a problem, and the storage of materials is difficult. However, for the visitors to the abbey it is an added interest to watch the embroiderers at work.

This group has also undertaken the making of 44 canvas-work cushions for the canons' stalls. These were designed by Pat Russell and measure 64 × 35 cm (25 × 14 in.). They are worked on canvas with ten threads to 2.5 cm (1 in.). They depict a shield in the middle, with a ribbon and scroll below and the name of the bishop. The surrounding roses and leaves on a

48 St Oswald; one of four hangings in Malpas parish church, worked in a wide range of canvas-work stitches.

49 St Werburga. Her thick plaits with braided ends hang freely down her dress, which is worked using a wide and imaginative range of stitches. The flowered border makes a charming frame.

blue background are worked in tramme gros point stitch using three strands of wool; two strands are used for the petit-point work.

The sedilia hangings, St Oswald's, Malpas, Cheshire

The beautiful parish church of St Oswald was built in the fifteenth century on the site of an earlier church. Four canvas-work hangings which were designed and worked by three members of the St Oswald's Needlework Group – Denise Bates (Mrs Rylands), Margaret Bradshaw and Dorothy Vickers – now hang in the stone niches of the sanctuary.

Three of the hangings depict saints, one of whom, St Oswald the king, is the patron saint of the church. The other two, St Chad and St Werburga, also have connections with the area; the former was a bishop of Lichfield, and the latter a princess and daughter of the king of Mercia, in later life the abbess of Ely. The design on the fourth hanging is an allegory taken from an early design found in a church in Rome.

The colours for the embroideries were care-fully chosen: royal reds and purples for St Oswald, and quiet greens and amethyst for the scholar-bishop. It took ten years to complete the four embroideries, which were finished in 1977. One of the workers, a farmer's wife, was able to take advantage of an enforced isolation and get on with the embroidery while confined to her farm during a foot-and-mouth epidemic.

A great deal of work obviously went into the researching of this project, and Malpas is very fortunate to have a professional painter in Denise Rylands, the wife of the rector. Her skills were put to advantage in what was to her a new medium of fabric and threads.

The Stourport deanery embroideries

Pamela Fedden, wife of the rural dean, had the idea that a set of embroidered panels should be

50 A detail from the Stourport Deanery embroideries, showing how interest can be added by using textural stitches for the background.

made to mark the 13th centenary of Worcester diocese; this happened to coincide with the rebuilding of Stourport church. The designs were made by the artist Mary Fedden, sister of the dean; this was her first embroidery design.

Daphne Nicholson, a member of the Practical Study Group of the Embroiderers' Guild, translated the designs into embroidery and supervised the work from the start. The project consists of 24 canvas-work panels, each measuring 76 × 48 cm (30 × 19 in.), worked in a variety of stitches. The panels are mounted in screens of four, surrounded by a wood frame with an embroidered border at the top and base. The border depicts heraldic motifs and flowers, and the influence of the Bayeux Tapestry is evident. Each screen measures about 168 × 112 cm (5 ft 6 in. × 3 ft 8 in.), and the panels feature aspects of each parish church, or of the village and its environment. For example, the village of Rochford is represented by sheep, Great Witley by the tower of its famous baroque parish church, and Kyre by its pool and water lilies.

The panels were worked entirely within the deanery by a team of approximately 80 men and women, aged between 16 and 75 years, led by some knowledgeable and experienced embroiderers. The work took two years from conception to completion. The panels are not signed, but a complete list of the workers is sewn to the back of each piece.

Some interesting facts and figures have been produced: each canvas measured 76 × 48 cm (30 × 19 in.) with 100 holes per square inch; this gives 57,000 holes per canvas, making 1,368,000 holes stitched in the complete embroidery!

7
Church kneelers

Forming a group to make church kneelers (also known as hassocks) is perhaps one of the most popular types of embroidery projects. The activity started in 1925, when Louisa Pesel came to live in Hampshire. She was an accomplished designer and embroiderer, having studied drawing and design under Lewis Day. In 1903 she was appointed designer to the Royal Hellenic Schools of Needlework and Lace in Athens, and worked there for five years, during which time she travelled widely, always with an eye for design and stitchery. On her return to England she lectured widely and worked for the Victoria and Albert Museum. In 1914, as 'an award of

honour in recognition of all her work for the study and revival of embroidery in England', she was presented by the Worshipful Company of Broderers with a gold chatelaine containing gold scissors, thimble, and needle case. In 1920 she became president of the Embroiderers' Guild when meetings restarted after the First World War.

In Winchester, Miss Pesel designed and supervised the cushions and kneelers for the bishop's private chapel which until then had been unfurnished; the work was executed by the Wolvesey Canvas Embroidery Guild. It was then suggested by the dean that a similar scheme

should be embarked upon for the cathedral, and to undertake this huge project the Winchester Cathedral Broderers were founded in 1931, financed by the Friends of the cathedral. This project seems to have been a daunting task. Designs were taken from the roof bosses and the wood carving in the choir, and a long period of experimental stitching was undertaken. The size of the venture was enormous: 360 kneelers, 96 alms bags, 34 long bench cushions and 62 stall cushions had to be made. During the war, when her embroiderers were employed on other tasks, Louisa Pesel was helped by the girls from the Atherley School, Southampton, then evacuated to the deanery, who worked on kneelers for the Lady Chapel. One of her most stalwart helpers was Catherine Little, whose sampler for the cathedral kneelers is shown in fig. 51. Louisa Pesel died in 1947, and at her funeral in the cathedral, a pall, which she had herself designed, was used for the first time.

Following the example and inspiration of Louisa Pesel at Winchester, many needle-women have joined forces on projects to beautify their churches, usually, initially, by refurbishing the kneelers.

Organizing a kneeler project

After a decision has been made that such a project should go ahead, the first step should be the formation of a committee. Ideally this should not be too large, but it could possibly include the wife of the incumbent, a treasurer to receive donations and keep the accounts and at least one skilled embroiderer with experience of canvas work to teach and guide the workers. Someone will be needed to hold the stock of canvas and wools and to allocate these to the workers, and to keep important records such as details of the date when each kneeler was started, and the names and addresses of the workers. It is also essential to involve someone with art training or knowledge of design work, though he or she need not necessarily be a member of the committee, but can be co-opted or commissioned to make the designs; if the designer has no experience of embroidery, he or she will need to work closely with the skilled embroiderer, who will be able to visualize the design in terms of stitchery. Depending upon the theme chosen, a local historian or school teacher can be very helpful in researching the subject.

Usually the Parochial Church Council will wish to see the designs, but it is really up to the vicar to give his approval, and his enthusiasm can do much to lift and encourage the work.

The costing of the project needs to be realistic, and it should not be overlooked that the kneelers may need to be professionally made up; quotations for this should be obtained. Plans must be made for fund raising; coffee mornings are a good way of raising money, and often parishioners can be persuaded to donate a kneeler in memory of a loved one. Workers must be recruited, and it is important to make sure at the outset that a sufficient number of parishioners are willing to take part and to give their time to finish a kneeler. An article should be put in the parish magazine or local paper, inviting those interested to come forward, even if they have little previous experience in embroidery. It helps to fix a target date by which a certain number of kneelers will be finished, and it is best to begin with the choir or a side chapel, rather than to be over-ambitious at the start.

In general, the more people involved, who can take a pride from being part of the project, the better, and the men of the parish should be encouraged to participate. I know several who do very fine canvas work, and there seems to have been a tradition in the navy for 'tapestry' as it is sometimes called.

A great deal of care and thought must go into the colour and design of the kneelers, as canvas work is very durable and they will be there for a long time. It is vital that they are thought of in relation to the church as a whole, complementing and enhancing the existing church furnishings, the stained glass and architectural features. The introduction of colour can brighten dark places and please the eye. The most successful projects are those where a good, simple theme is carried throughout, with a single colour-scheme predominant for the background and sides of the kneelers, though this can be varied. There are books available with designs for kneelers, but it is much more satisfying to make your own designs, and originality in the theme and use of stitches can create a work that is unique and complementary to your church.

The size and thickness of the kneelers must be

51 A sampler made by Catherine Little for the Winchester Cathedral kneeler project organized by Louisa Pesel.

decided. Should they hang upon the back of the pew in front? If so a D-ring must be attached. The kneelers have been stolen from some churches, and for kneelers which are to remain on the floor, a method can be devised for threading them on to a cord attached to the pew, though this does not look very attractive.

Before embarking on the kneelers themselves, it is wise for the volunteers first to work a sampler to try out different and unfamiliar stitches, the use of which can greatly enhance the work and give life and texture to a very simple design or background. The sampler could be in the form of a pin cushion, and it can also serve to assess the skills of group members. Again, I would stress that it is essential for the project to have available someone with training in design, who has an eye for colour and can visualize the scheme as a whole. All the expense,

time, and hard work can be in vain if the basic designs are poor.

It is very useful to keep a scrapbook to contain ideas, postcards, cuttings from colour supplements and similar relevant material, and perhaps also a photographic record of the kneelers as they are completed.

Design

Having decided upon the size and shape of the kneelers, and the overall theme, the basic design must be worked out. This could be an interesting geometrical repeating pattern, or varying motifs such as crosses, doves, fish, or heraldic devices, set within a shape or border common to all the kneelers. Colour combinations can be interchanged and stitches varied in order to

52 A kneeler from Aldeburgh church, Suffolk, showing the effect of changing the direction of stitches.

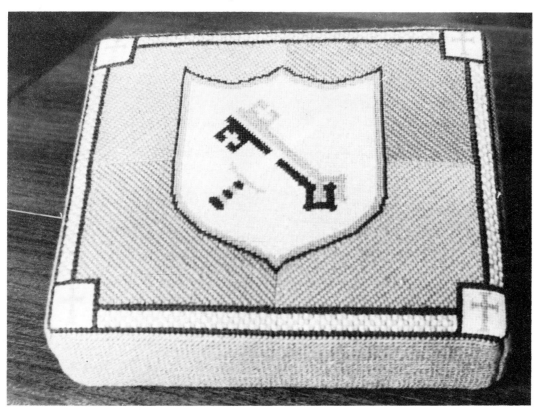

avoid uniformity and to provide additional interest. Also, the embroiderers should be encouraged to exercise their individual creative ability while working within an overall standard specification.

Designs must be looked at in the church, both in natural and in artificial light, and they must first be thought of in terms of colour and composition, then in terms of stitchery. A large, plain area can be brought to life by changing the direction of the stitches, or by using different stitches and combinations of stitches. This is well illustrated by the Abbots Ann kneelers, where the background is worked in Byzantine stitch combined with a chequered-pattern stitch. This approach also makes the work much less monotonous for the embroiderers.

Transferring the design to canvas

Once the design is completed, it then has to be transferred to the canvas. To place a design on canvas, I find it easier to use a light-box or light-table (as described on page 18). Use hard pencil or a waterproof paint to trace the design on to the canvas. Oil paint thinned with turpentine can be used, but make sure that the paint is completely dry before starting work. Alternatively, acrylic paint which dries immediately, or waterproof ink are suitable. Never use a ball-point pen as when the canvas is completed and dampened to be stretched, any non-waterproof ink will come through and stain the wool. A straightforward design, drawn on graph paper, each square representing a square of the canvas mesh, can be transferred by simply counting the corresponding number of squares on the canvas.

Canvas

There are two kinds of canvas. Single-thread is most widely used as it will take all the stitches normally required and is easy to count. Double or Penelope canvas is used for trammed, tent, or cross stitch. The size of the canvas is gauged by the number of threads to 2.5 cm (1 in.); either 10 or 18 threads to 2.5 cm (1 in.) is usual for kneelers. It pays to use the best-quality linen canvas, as kneelers have to stand up to hard wear over the years. When calculating the amount of canvas that will be needed, allow for a margin of at least 5 cm (2 in.) around the embroidery. If the canvas is to be worked by hand, the edges must be bound.

Wools

Crewel wool is very fine, and the number of strands used can be varied according to the size of the canvas and type of stitch; mixed strands of different colours can also be used to give a subtle effect. It is cheaper to buy your wool by the hank, not by the skein. It is wise to ensure that enough wool is purchased to complete the work in hand, as there is no guarantee that the colours can be exactly matched. It is difficult to estimate the quantities of wool required as the amount used will vary according to the variety of stitches employed, and the neatness of the individual embroiderer!

Tapestry wool corresponds to 4-ply knitting yarn, and can be used for medium-gauge double or single canvas. It is wise to buy moth-proofed wool. Thrums, which can be obtained from carpet factories, are hard-wearing and excellent for the coarser canvases.

Needles

The correct needle to use is a tapestry needle. This has a rounded point which will slip easily through the holes without splitting the canvas. Needles are available in various sizes from gauge 24 to 18 (the largest). The needle must be the right size to match the size of canvas being used, so that the wool passes through the hole without fraying.

Frames

It is a great advantage to use a frame as it keeps the canvas evenly stretched, and if supported leaves both hands free. A higher standard of evenness will be achieved, and the work keeps its shape.

Use an oblong frame, not a round hoop or tambour frame which is only suitable for small, fine work. Embroidery frames can be expensive to buy, but as an alternative you can use an old picture frame or a stretcher for an oil painting, with drawing-pins (thumb tacks) to fasten the canvas. An improvised frame can be made fairly cheaply using broom handles for the rollers.

1 Part of a wall-hanging designed by Elizabeth Ashurst for the Chailey Heritage Craft School for Physically Handicapped Children. The hanging was worked by members of the Kingston Adult Education Centre Workshop.

2 Squares, before mounting, from the Pebble Mill Heritage Tapestry, organized by Kaffe Fassett.

3 A detail from the New Forest embroidery, designed by the author and worked by local embroiderers.

4 One of a set of four copes designed by Jane Lemon and made by the Sarum Group for Salisbury Cathedral.

5 The hood of one of the set of five copes designed by Barbara Siedlecka for Winchester Cathedral. The copes were made by Nancy Kimmins, Moyra McNeill and students of the Beckenham Adult Education Centre.

6 A canvas-work kneeler showing the symbol of St Mark the Evangelist – a winged lion; one of a set of kneelers in St Mary's church, Nantwich.

7 Four kneelers depicting musical instruments, from the choir stalls of St Mary's, Nantwich.

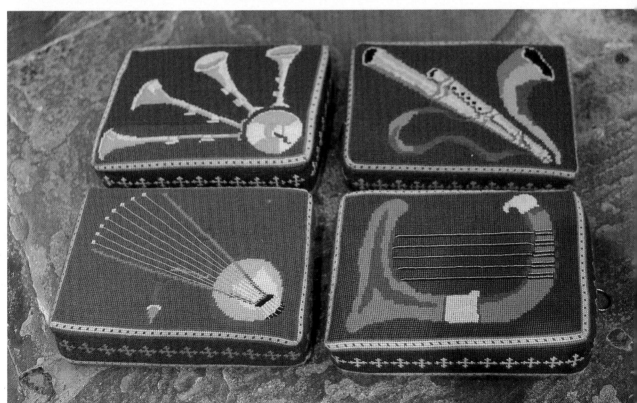

8 Detail of a kneeler for the high altar at Salisbury Cathedral; designed by the author and made by eight members of the Sarum Group.

9 'Elements in Salvation'; one of four hangings in St Alban's Cathedral, designed by Sister Regina of Cockfosters and made by St Alban's Cathedral Embroidery Group. *(J. J. Brookes)*

10 'Autumn'; one side of the screen designed by Pauline Allett and made by members of the Northamptonshire branch of the Embroiderers' Guild.

11 'Summer'; a hanging from Crestwood School,
Eastleigh, Hampshire; made in ripped nylon applied
by machine.

Before dressing the frame, first bind the sides of the canvas; a length of string can be threaded through the binding to give strength to the sides. Mark both the centre of the canvas, and the centre of the webbing attached to the roller of the frame. Pin and line up the canvas to the webbing, then, using strong thread, overcast top and bottom. Place side pieces through the slots in the rollers of the frame, and insert pegs to keep the canvas taut. The sides are then laced with thin string to the frame, thus pulling the fabric taut.

Instructions for the needleworkers

I suggest that the needleworkers are given a page of written instructions, so that those lacking in confidence and skill have something to which they can refer. This should include the name and telephone number of the skilled embroiderer who will help out with technical advice when needed, a list of the stitches required, and any other information that will make for the unity of the project.

The use of stitches

Diagrams of stitches are not included in this book as there are many works devoted to canvas-work stitches; I suggest, however, that very long stitches which might catch and pull, or pronounced raised stitches, are not suitable for kneelers which must be hard-wearing and durable.

Tent and cross stitches are not the only simple stitches. Florentine, gobelin and bricking make smooth surfaces, while cross, double-cross, and rice stitch can be worked in two colours or tones and are more textured. Some stitches combine better than others. Stitches with definite directional textures are most effective, particularly if used to provide contrast between different areas of plain colour. Make sure that your stitches cover the canvas.

53 A detail of the high-altar kneeler of Salisbury Cathedral, designed by the author. Many different stitches were used for the fillings.

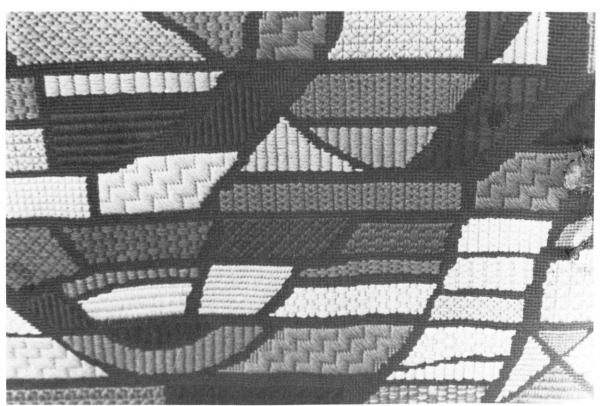

54 A kneeler from Abbots Ann, Hampshire, showing a simple design enhanced by stitches.

Arranging the work on the canvas

It is preferable to make the embroidery all in one piece, leaving four lines of unworked canvas between the top and sides so that the bend can be whipped in long-legged cross stitch. This is both stronger, uses less canvas, and saves time and effort in comparison with the alternative of working separate top and sides; the latter is only to be recommended when it is necessary for the top and sides to be worked by different embroiderers.

Working in sections to be joined

If a large altar-rail kneeler has been divided into sections to be worked by several people, and is subsequently to be joined, make sure the sections are placed so that the grain of the threads all goes in the same direction, as most canvas has more threads in one direction than in the other. Also, where there has to be a join, try to make it at a point where it shows the least, along a change of colour. In my design for the kneeler for the Salisbury Cathedral high-altar rail, knowing that it would be worked in three parts, I placed dark bars across the ends where the joins would come. Fortunately, these corresponded with the lead bars of the stained-glass window which had provided the inspiration for the design.

Note
When the embroidery is finished do *not* trim the canvas until after it has been stretched, and do *not* iron.

Stretching

The completed work will need to be stretched. You will require a trestle table or something

74

similar to work upon, some copper tacks or rustless drawing-pins (these can be kept for this use) to hold the canvas in position, and a set square to ensure that the corners are at right angles.

First, place some layers of blotting paper or newspaper over the table. To stretch the canvas squarely, nail the selvedge edge of the canvas to a straight side of the table or board. Then pull the other three sides into position and nail in place, ensuring that the canvas is evenly stretched and that all the corners are square. It may need some trial and error, and hard pulling, to get the canvas back into its proper shape.

Finally, the work must be throughly dampened with a sponge; use a dabbing, not a rubbing, motion. This will soften the gum or size in the canvas, and when left to dry over a period of one to two weeks, the canvas threads will reset in the correct position.

Preparing the kneelers for making-up

The initial stages of making up can be done by the embroiderers. If the top and sides have been worked separately, these must first be joined. First cut out, leaving a good 2.5 cm (1 in.)

margin for the turning. Then herringbone the turning to the back of the work, leaving three lines of unworked canvas thread exposed beyond the embroidery. The top, sides and corners are joined by working long-legged cross stitch over the two edges of unworked canvas.

If the kneeler has been worked in one piece, then there will be four lines of canvas left unworked between top and sides. First fold a side under the top and stitch along the fold with long-legged cross stitch; proceed similarly for the tops of the other three sides. At the corners the spare canvas can either be cut, or, if not too bulky, folded flat and left inside, and the corner seams worked down, also using long-legged cross stitch.

To cover the edges adequately, several strands of crewel wool will be required; this makes for a strong joint similar to piping.

55 Kneeler construction: how to make up and stitch the corners of a kneeler worked in one piece, using long-legged cross stitch over lines of unworked canvas.

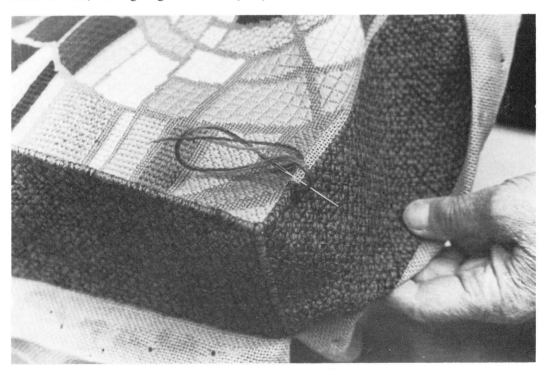

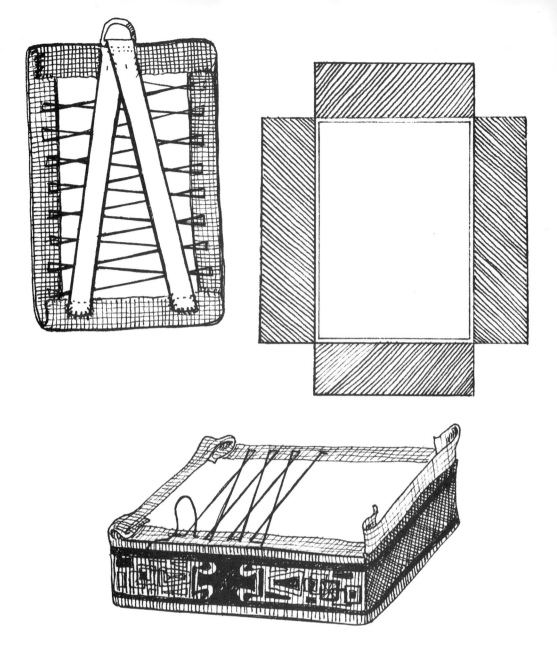

Making up

The kneelers are now ready to be made-up; they can be sent to a specialist upholsterer, but this may be expensive. Alternatively, it is sometimes possible to enlist the help and interest of a local upholsterer who will be prepared to show how this work should be done.

There are various materials which can be used for the pad or filling. Depending upon the size and thickness of the kneeler, and the degree of hardness required, different materials or combinations of materials are used.

A typical filling might be rubber latex (this should be cut with a sharp knife), with several layers of carpet felt on each side, compressed within a calico cover. Plastic foam, which is less dense than rubber latex, needs to be more compressed. In the past, horsehair was generally used, or sawdust, which tended to be heavy.

The made-up pad will need to be slightly larger than the embroidered canvas cover, as it

56 Four very striking kneelers from Nantwich church, depicting local architecture.

is to be further compressed in fitting. This is achieved by placing the cover over the pad, turning over the canvas margins, and lacing these across the bottom.

Next, if the kneeler is to be hung, the webbing with the D-ring threaded on must be stitched in place (see diagram). Finally, a rectangle of upholsterer's linen or black glazed cotton is stitched neatly with strong thread to cover the bottom of the kneeler.

Kneeler project at St Peter's Church, Milton Lilbourne, Wiltshire

The following account of the project was provided by Mrs Chetwynd-Talbot:

'Our village church has had little attention to its furnishings since the beginning of the century. After making pulpit falls, collecting bags, burse and veil, and remaking the altar frontals, I thought a village scheme for kneelers would be

learn the basics of setting up and marking a canvas. The stitches to be used and the designs were chosen by each individual. One of the group made up cheap slat frames from pieces of timber and broom handles. A number of kind people subscribed a small sum for a kneeler in memory of a friend or relative, and we were off.

'We felt it very important to work to a colour scheme, and as our red carpet is the most dominating colour in the church, we chose two reds for the background and sides, and a variety of golds for the margins. From kneelers we have expanded to a more ambitious project, a 488 cm (16 ft) runner for the altar rail. This has been worked in seven sections and joined up. Amongst our workers are two men, one of whom had never before held a canvas needle, let alone worked out a design on graph paper and translated it on to canvas.

'Although our two dozen kneelers to date have taken a year to complete, we are now all enthusiastic canvas workers, who will continue the good work, and, we hope, inspire others to join. Each kneeler bears the year of completion on the side panel, and in some cases the name or names of those in whose memory they have been worked, and inside the polythene lining is the name of the worker.'

Aldeburgh kneelers

The Aldeburgh kneelers are simple in design. They all have the same border, and are decorated with a centre motif of a saint's emblem such as St Luke's boat and St Peter's cross; also included are fish, flowers and local birds including the avocet and the curlew. The dark-gold background is worked in diagonal Florentine stitch.

The church is ornate, with dark pews, a certain amount of brass, and a very modern John Piper window, a memorial to Benjamin Britten, so the colours of the kneelers had to be rather restrained.

Few of those who embarked on this project had previously done any canvas work, but under the guidance of Catherine Benn, who had experience of working in women's organizations, the project went ahead. Not only church people were involved, and someone remarked 'Why was it that the first five kneelers to be finished had all been done by heathens?'

both fun and interesting. Curiously enough, at my first attempt at recruiting, I had an almost universal reaction of "Oh, but I can't do embroidery" or "I have only done canvas work from kits."

'Fortunately for the village we have in our midst a professional embroiderer who has recently retired from conservation work at Hampton Court. We decided that for a village project it was essential to keep costs down to a minimum, so opted for the work to be done in carpet thrums on a canvas of ten threads to 2.5 cm (1 in.). Together we chose colours and stitches, and six designs around the theme of St Peter, our patronal saint. Of course wool and canvas were limiting both in stitches and designs. Also, we had inexperienced workers.

'We held four classes for the volunteers to

Pew runner, St Mary and All Saints church, Ellingham, Hampshire

The church at Ellingham is most lovingly cared for. Here a group of 25 embroiderers have worked over a period of five years to complete kneelers and 26 pew runners. The designs consist of the emblems of the saints, alternating with the lily of St Mary, the Madonna Lily, which represents the church's dedication.

The detail in fig. 57 shows the fish and ring of St Kentigern or Mungo, who is best remembered for the legend associated with the symbol. King Roderick gave a ring to his queen, who passed it to her lover, one of the king's knights. When out hunting, Roderick and the knight rested on the bank of the Clyde, and in his sleep the knight stretched out his hand and revealed the ring. The king, holding himself in check, quietly slipped the ring off the finger of the guilty man, and threw it in the river. On returning home, the king asked the queen for

57 A detail from a pew runner from Ellingham church, where all the pews have runners as well as kneelers; worked by Lady Caroline Agar.

the ring. Unable to produce it, she was about to be executed, but was granted a stay of three days. She consulted St Kentigern, and he, remembering that his own mother, whom he greatly loved, had borne him out of wedlock, felt sorry for the Queen and prayed for her. The ring was found in the belly of a salmon caught in the Clyde, returned to the Queen, and all was forgiven.

The pew runner was worked by Lady Caroline Agar.

The high-altar kneelers, Salisbury Cathedral

The design (by the author) for the long high-altar kneeler was inspired by the new east window by Gabriel Loire. The theme of the window was the Prisoners of Conscience, united across all frontiers by the stand for truth, from the time of Christ until the present day.

In tone, the colours range from light yellows and golds in the centre, to shades of blue and violet towards the sides, with dashes of scarlet and violet which echo the colours in the window above, and also pick up exactly the colours in the altar frontal designed by Jane Lemon. The designs, painted in very bright colours, looked extremely garish in my workroom, but when seen in the cathedral, they fall into place, complementing the altar frontal and linking the scheme as a whole.

For convenience, the 914 cm (30 ft) kneeler was divided into eight sections, each of which was to be worked by a member of the Sarum Group. The embroiderers were given a list of stitches, including Byzantine, long-and-short, mosaic and different cross stitches; the sides were worked in rice stitch in two tones of blue. I painted the outline of the design on the canvas in waterproof, black acrylic paint, and then, as a colour-guide, looped coloured strands of Appleton's crewel wool through each section. I found this method far better and quicker than painting in the colours, as the canvas soaks up the paint and it is impossible to match the shades correctly.

58 Detail of an altar-rail kneeler made by the Mothers' Union for St Margaret's Chapel, Salisbury Cathedral.

The finished sections were joined to make two long and two shorter sections. As the existing kneeler cushion was badly misshapen, it was decided that it should be replaced, and the completed work was sent to professional upholsterers to be made up.

In my first design the leaded outlines were in black, but subsequently it was decided to change them to shades of blue, very dark at the sides but lightening towards the centre. This resulted from looking at the design in the cathedral, and discussing it with the dean, Jane Lemon, and members of the Group; this was a most helpful and important meeting, which demonstrates the importance of looking at designs *in situ*, in relation to existing furnishings and lighting.

Kneelers for the Chapel of St Margaret of Scotland, Salisbury Cathedral

These kneelers were worked by Evelyn Copp, Myrtle Tanner and Jacqueline Avery, members of the Mothers' Union, which adopted this chapel. The Scottish thistles are the home for the native birds of Scotland, including the goldcrest and the dipper.

8
Chairs, stools and tablecloths

Canvas work is an excellent technique for a group project, and the opportunity should not be missed to re-cover antique chairs or stools, which may enhance some fine public room and be seen and enjoyed by many people. The organization is much the same as for a church-kneeler project; it is wise to work samplers first, as was done by all those taking part in the Leeds Castle chair-backs project.

A tablecloth may be designed to cover a table used by a committee, perhaps raised on a platform or stage; a smart cloth adds greatly to the image of any institute or society. This is a perfect project for an inexperienced group. A cloth must be made to fit the table and touch the ground at the front and sides. Gone are the days of little white cloths with lazy-daisy chains. Design a cloth using a fabric of darkish tone, and break the design into sections which can be worked by individuals. The cloth made by Romsey WI is an excellent example.

The Leeds Castle chair-backs

A set of 50 chair-backs was worked in 1980 by members of the local Embroiderers' Guild. The chairs were made in oak for the banqueting hall of Leeds Castle, Kent, to a design by Barry Mazur. The emblem of the castle, a knight in armour brandishing a sword, is embroidered on the chair-backs; the initials of those who worked each chair is included in the right-hand corner of the canvas. The seats are upholstered in a dark-brown wool fabric which matches well the background of the chair-backs.

Julia Hickman translated the design on to canvas with 14 threads per 2.5 cm (1 in.) using different stitches, which make the simple design less flat and much more interesting than it would have been had only one or two stitches been used. All the participants first worked a small sample to test their ability in reading a complex chart, and to make sure they had mastered all the stitches involved.

The result of this ambitious project is very pleasing, and contributes to the very high standard of the fabric in this beautiful and historic building. The castle was bequeathed by the Hon. Lady Baillie to a charitable trust for the promotion of outstanding achievement in medical science, as well as to preserve the beauty of the building and its grounds for the enjoyment of the public.

59 A design for the Leeds Castle chair project (1980).

60 A sampler by Julia Hickman to try out stitches before embarking on the projects.

61 Detail from one of the 50 chair-backs, Leeds Castle.

The Malmesbury House chairs

Patricia Champness, a professional designer, made the designs for a set of eight chairs which were worked in tent stitch by some 30 members from nine branches of the Embroiderers' Guild.

This project was commissioned by a gentleman who lives in one of the beautiful houses in the Cathedral Close, Salisbury.

62 One of a set of eight chairs worked by members of nine branches of the Embroiderers' Guild; designed by Patricia Champness for a private house.

84

Florentine stool-tops, Palace of Holyroodhouse

The Scottish Women's Rural Institutes decided to work a piece of embroidery to commemorate the Queen's silver-wedding anniversary, and they asked permission of Her Majesty to present a set of coverings for the stools in the portrait gallery of the Palace of Holyroodhouse. In 1970 a small deputation visited the palace, and the Queen chose the colours to match new yellow curtains which were being made for the banqueting hall. A Florentine design was selected, to be worked in crewel wool, with filo floss to give highlights.

Eleven stools were covered by the 33 county federations, each working one-third of a canvas; their names were embroidered on the part of the canvas that forms the turn-over so as not to be visible, but on each stool a small plaque reads 'Worked by Scottish Women's Rural Institutes and Presented to Her Majesty Queen Elizabeth and His Royal Highness the Duke of Edinburgh on the occasion of their Silver Wedding 20 November 1972'.

A deputation made up of one representative from each federation had the thrill of going to the palace for the presentation to the Queen in person, and of seeing the completed stools in place in the window embrasures.

63 One of the stools in the Palace of Holyroodhouse, worked by the Scottish Women's Rural Institutes for HM the Queen's Silver Wedding (1972). (*Scottish Women's Rural Institutes*)

64 A breakfast set presented as a Silver Wedding present to HM the Queen by members of the Scottish Women's Rural Institutes. (*Scottish Women's Rural Institutes*)

Breakfast set presented to Her Majesty the Queen

This was worked by several members of the Scottish Women's Rural Institutes from a winning design submitted by a member of the Institutes. It is worked in white thread on yellow linen, and was presented to the Queen as a more personal gift to commemorate her silver wedding.

Romsey Women's Institute tablecloth

This project was organized by June Thorp and the cloth was made by 18 members of the Romsey Women's Institute to fit exactly over a 244 cm (8 ft) table. All the workers' signatures are embroidered on the inside.

The 30 cm (12 in.) panels on the front and sides represent various Women's Institute activities, and were individually designed by those who worked them. They are mainly worked in machine appliqué with some hand embroidery to embellish the detail. The cloth is green cotton, bordered with two lines in two shades of red.

Perhaps this will inspire others to make interesting tablecloths for the chairwoman and officers to shelter behind at meetings.

The Women's Institute tablecloth for headquarters

This magnificent tablecloth was designed by Nancy Kimmins, who is an experienced teacher of embroidery, and was trained at the Royal School of Needlework.

As the coat of arms of the Women's Institute

65 The Romsey Women's Institute tablecloth,
organized by June Thorp. The panels are worked
in machine appliqué with some hand embroidery.

66 Herons and heraldic emblems in canvas work
to be applied to the Women's Institute tablecloth.
(*Nancy Kimmins*)

was to be used to cover the front, advice was sought from the College of Arms to ensure that the design was heraldically correct. The design was divided into sections, each worked on fine canvas using a variety of stitches by members of the Polhill and Orpington Priory branch of the Institute. The canvas-work sections were then cut out and stitched down on the dark green woollen furnishing fabric of the tablecloth. Cords were stitched around the outlines to make a neat finish.

This large throwover cloth is used at the Institute's annual general meetings, held at the Royal Albert Hall, London.

67 The Women's Institute tablecloth. (*Nancy Kimmins*)

9
Screens and banners

The Northamptonshire screen

In 1974, on hearing that the Embroiderers' Guild wanted each branch to donate an embroidered item or heirloom for auction to raise funds, one of the members of the Northamptonshire branch, Mrs Grace Barlow, suggested a screen that might be used; it had four panels to be embroidered on each side.

Miss Paulene Allett, a trained artist and designer, was asked to produce a design for a group project and to co-ordinate the work. She first designed a flower motif, thinking that everyone could work on individual flowers and leaves; however, feeling that the design should have a Northamptonshire flavour, she prepared a second design showing the countryside and houses, and this was chosen by the branch. The design was to be repeated on both sides of the screen, showing the scene in autumn on one side and in spring on the other. A basic background fabric was used to give unity throughout, with added accessories to create the seasonal colour changes. (See colour plate 10.)

Next, a full-scale tonal representation was made of the design to establish the four panels, to set down the basic lines, and to balance the areas of interest. Assorted papers, some printed, were used to indicate the density of tone and/or degree of pattern required. The members traced off the area they had elected to work; they were asked to pay particular attention to tone and line so that the pieces would link together. It took considerable organization to ensure that no pieces were missed or duplicated.

The screen is 183 cm (6 ft) high, each panel being 61 cm (2 ft) wide. The background is a soft-green hessian mounted on washed calico (it is important to shrink the calico). All members pooled scraps from dressmaking, and these were allocated at the same time as the designs, to help to ensure that the colour-scheme was closely followed. Each member was given a free choice of method of work; some methods combined more than one type of embroidery, and as the pieces were completed, it was fascinating to see the different approaches and methods used.

Individual pieces were worked on cotton scrim so that, when cut out, a hem could be turned under without bulk when mounting on the screen. Each piece was hemmed in place and fields were fitted in between in suitable colours, embroidered as necessary. A number of the larger trees were machine-embroidered on vanishing muslin by one of the members; these were very successful, except for one that vanished completely when ironed with an over-hot iron! A hedge top was done in free canvas work using many stitches; a gate was designed and worked in pillow lace by Miss Joan Savage.

The home of Mrs Joyce Tailby was used as a base for the entire project, with members calling in to add more stitches to the screen. It took about eight months to complete, during which time the tonal design, mounted on the screen frame, stood in the hall for reference, while the work progressed on two large frames on trestles. The panels were gradually completed, and all eight were re-assembled and framed by Mr Tailby. After a brief appearance on Wellingborough television, the screen was packed and dispatched to the Embroiderers' Guild, and was subsequently sold to an American for £500, the highest price paid for any item in the whole fund-raising effort.

The screen was an absorbing project with a much greater value than merely fund raising.

68 A detail of a cockerel from the Girl Guides' banner, before making up; designed by Nancy Kimmins. (*Nancy Kimmins*)

Division of the Standard of the Orpington division of the Girl Guides' Association

This banner was designed and organized by Nancy Kimmins. The design strictly adheres to the heraldic rules of colour on metal and metal on colour, and it is worked using simple appliqué with a little embroidery, all sewn by hand. The two sides of the banner were made separately and then joined back to back. The motifs were chosen by the girls themselves, and the work was carried out by their mothers, who had varied needlework abilities, mostly in dressmaking. The highly professional finish owes much to the experience and knowledge of the designer.

When making a banner, the weight is an important consideration. Jockey silk, if it can be obtained, is excellent as it is very light, but poplin is perfectly adequate and comes in a very wide range of colours. Do not forget that a banner needs to be colour-fast in case it is caught in the rain.

Banner for the Lord Provost's car, Edinburgh

In 1984 the Edinburgh branch of the Embroiderers' Guild decided that it would like to contribute a piece of embroidery to the city. As a start, it was suggested by the Lord Provost's Office that a small banner should be embroidered for the Lord Provost's car, to be used on major ceremonial occasions and to replace the printed-fabric banner usually displayed.

69 The completed banner. (*Nancy Kimmins*)

After consultation with the Court of the Lord Lyon, the Edinburgh city arms, a castle on a rock, were drawn out on white silk. The three turrets and the rock made four natural units of work. It was decided to make each side of the banner separately, so there were eight units of work to be allocated among eight volunteers, all of whom had first worked a test piece.

The embroidery is in long-and-short stitch in one strand of French stranded silk. Each side of the banner was mounted on a frame, so that it could easily be handed from worker to worker.

The silver fringe is made of some 800 individually made cords, 5 cm (2 in.) long. Two volunteers shared this part of the project and twisted the cords semi-mechanically, one using a hand drill and the other a lacemaker's bobbin-winder, to speed the process. The cords were laid on double-sided tape to keep the fringe even. Another volunteer made up the finished banner.

This project took several months to complete, and was organized by Muriel Tilling.

10
The work of Judy Chicago

'The Dinner Party'

'I have brought these women together, invited them to dinner, so to speak, in order that we might hear what they have to say, and see the range and beauty of their heritage.' (Judy Chicago)

'The Dinner Party' certainly is a very significant and important epic statement. When Judy Chicago embarked on her own upon its creation, she did not imagine how the project would develop, and that it would eventually become a group project requiring many helping hands.

Judy Chicago is one of America's foremost feminist artists. 'The Dinner Party' was conceived as a work of art symbolizing the achievements of women in Western civilization. It consists of an open, triangular table measuring 14 m (46 ft 6 in.) on each side, standing on a large triangular floor of porcelain tiles inscribed in gold lustre with the names of 999 women of achievement. The table is covered by a white cloth edged in gold, with 13 place-settings on each side, making a total of 39 places. The number 13 refers to the number present at the Last Supper, and also to the number of members in a witches' coven; the number 13 thus has both a positive and a negative meaning, consistent with the dual meaning of 'The Dinner Party'.

Each place is set with a 35 cm (14 in.) painted china plate, representing a period of Western civilization as well as a woman or mythological figure, a gold ceramic chalice, a knife, fork and spoon, and a napkin edged with gold. Each setting rests on an embroidered runner, which lies across the table hanging over the front and back, with the name of the woman represented embroidered on the front of each runner. The plates and their settings together signify the identity of the woman portrayed, her aspirations, and the period in history.

The runners on the first wing of the table cover the period from pre-history to the time of Rome, the second wing from the beginning of Christianity to the Reformation, and the third wing from the American Revolution to the Women's Revolution. The names of the women are all identical in size, colour, placement and technique. They are all worked in split stitch outlined in Japanese gold. The capitals are all illuminated.

The paintings of Queen Elizabeth I in her superbly embroidered dresses provided the inspiration for her runner. Traditional Elizabethan floral motifs are combined with blackwork fillings, and embellished with gold threads, cords and pearls.

Initially, the table-runners were thought of merely as a background for the plates and the designs were painted on cotton fabric in order to visualize the concept, but as the workers' knowledge and interest in embroidery grew, interpreting the designs into threads and stitches became an exciting challenge. The embroidery then became an important part of the whole project, and a sample book was made.

Embroidery frames were specially designed by Millie Stein, and constructed of hardwood so that they would not warp. They were large enough to take the white linen runner so that it could be worked and viewed as an overall picture, without rolling up and obscuring part

70 'The Dinner Party', designed by Judy Chicago. (*Judy Chicago – Diehard Productions*)

93

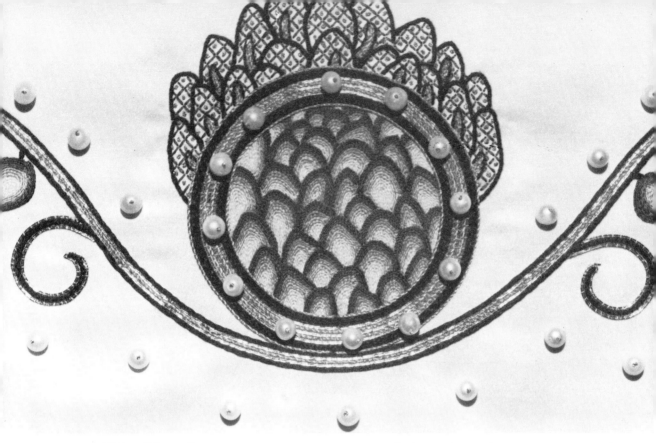

71 Detail from 'The Dinner Party'. (*Judy Chicago – Diehard Productions*)

of the design. The frames were mounted on stands, and could be tilted so that more than one person could work at the same time. The linen was laced to the frame in the traditional manner, but was stretched and positioned to a great degree of accuracy, using rulers and set-squares to check and position the fabric. The designs were carefully redrawn by Judy on blue-lined graph paper, then taped on to the linen, and, with the aid of a specially built light-table, traced with blue pencil on to the linen.

Some of the runners were designed with particular techniques in mind, others were developed after much research and experimentation by the embroiderer. The finished runners were finally lined and backed with white linen. The signatures of everyone who had made a significant contribution were embroidered on the back of each runner in order not to perpetuate the tradition of anonymity so prevalent in needlework.

For about eighteen months Judy Chicago worked on the project on her own before looking for help. Among the first to volunteer her time was Susan Hill, who had a good knowledge of needlework, although she was not at that time a skilled embroiderer. It was Susan who suggested that it would be almost impossible to embroider the long tablecloths, and it was her idea to make runners for each place setting. Susan became the head of needlework for the project, and to improve her embroidery techniques she joined a group of traditional embroiderers working one day a week. Judy studied china painting for the plates which were to be in relief – an exceedingly difficult technique.

As the number of volunteers increased, a set of studio rules evolved to protect the work-time. One evening a week was set aside for discussions, lectures and pot-luck dinners, when Judy made herself available to answer questions. Consciousness-raising groups were formed and met weekly to work out any problems, and to provide a sense of involvement between project members. Teams evolved not only in needlework and ceramics, but also in research, graphics and photography.

Every aspect of the project was considered in great depth before each step was taken. After extensive research into textile conservation, all the fabrics and threads were tested by washing and by dry-cleaning to remove excess dye and to determine the best way to clean them. Records were kept with instructions for each runner, as a guide for future maintenance and restoration. Methods had to be devised for securing 'The Dinner Party' to the table in order to prevent theft and damage. The runners had to be strapped to the tablecloth, the napkins sewn down, and all ceramic pieces bolted in position.

To participate in such a project is a very rewarding experience; to be exposed to the quest for excellence, to be part of a team and to communicate and work in harmony, learning from others, is something few people have the opportunity to share in; however, it does take a great deal of energy, dedication and commitment to keep such a large project moving over a period of time until completion.

'The Dinner Party' cost $250,000 in materials, and the funding of the project all came from the earnings of Judy Chicago over a period of five years. $60,000 was received in assorted grants and donations from people all over America, and millions of dollars' worth of labour was freely given. The responsibility for fund-raising and public relations was assumed by Diane Gelon, a history of art student. The project was completed in 1979 after five years' work by over 400 people. It has been exhibited in San Francisco, Houston, Boston, Brooklyn, Cleveland, Chicago, Montreal, Toronto, Atlanta, Calgary, Edinburgh and London.

'The Birth Project'

Judy Chicago has now channelled her undoubted energy into yet another huge group project of a different kind to 'The Dinner Party'. The idea of 'The Birth Project' began when Chicago, who has no children, was researching for 'The Dinner Party', and realized that there were no birth images in Western Art. Declaring that 'If men had babies, there would be thousands of images of the crowning', she determined to introduce the subject to the art world.

The needleworkers, who number over 100, pledge to work for at least ten hours each week, undertaking to follow Chicago's specifications completely, even unpicking when the work is not to her liking. They are unpaid, but enjoy the opportunity of working with an artist of stature. They all work in their own homes, and Chicago visits them in periodic regional reviews to assess the work and progress.

Although the project is entirely Chicago's concept, she emphatically declines to take all the credit, encouraging her needleworkers to the fore, and believing that in this work the boundary between artist and artisan blurs. The embroiderers must take aesthetic decisions in translating the designs into fabric and thread.

This mammoth undertaking, conceived in 1980, will bring together over 100 works to be exhibited in libraries, birth centres and colleges, as well as museums in America, and already some have been exhibited. The embroideries are the property of 'Through the Flower', a non-profit making corporation.

Chicago resolves not to show more than six pieces at a time: 'If people see any more they go full tilt, and can't take anything in at all.' Each completed piece of work is displayed in a 8.5 m (28 ft) long exhibit unit that includes the names and photographs of all the workers, with entries from their journals and letters, information on the materials and techniques employed, and other related historical and literary material.

11
Quilts

In the past five years there has been a great revival of interest in quilting in Britain. The Quilters' Guild was founded in August 1979 and now has a membership of over 2,000; there are well over 200 regional groups throughout Britain, holding workshops and classes.

Patchwork, appliqué and quilting were all invented out of necessity rather than for decorative use. Patchwork was first made by piecing together small scraps of material to make something serviceable at a time when fabrics were precious and hard to come by. Appliqué is made by stitching fabric shapes on to an existing ground, possibly to cover worn or holed fabrics, and only later became decorative work. Quilting is the stitching together of two layers of fabric with a layer of wadding or fleece sandwiched between, and is a most practical form of insulation, both for garments and bed quilts.

These techniques have all been used since the earliest times. Quilted coats have been worn by soldiers from the eleventh century up to the present day. In the seventeenth century, quilting was widely used on all types of clothes, and in the eighteenth century fine bedspreads were frequently made of plain cream silk which was both quilted and embroidered.

The finest examples of patchwork and quilting were then found to be in America, where they were taken by English and Dutch settlers between 1775 and 1885. Many different types of quilts for different occasions were produced in America by women meeting together in each other's houses.

Quilting has traditionally been a communal activity, with groups of women meeting up for quilting bees. Friendship quilts were made, with each section being worked by a different member in patchwork or appliqué, and finally the whole piece would be quilted.

Patchwork

Patchwork squares can be designed by individuals working to a common theme, or as samplers of different types of traditional patchwork design, but careful planning is needed to make the design effective as a whole. Advantage must be made of the grouping of dark and light, printed and plain fabrics of stripes or gingham checks; colours, which are best restricted to a limited range of two or three, should be carefully juxtaposed. The friendship hanging made for Julia Walker's new kitchen is a lovely example of patchwork; the colours are limited, but the squares are the personal expression of those who made them.

Almost any fabrics can be used, but finely woven materials, which tend not to fray and can be easily folded over the template, are best. Finely woven cotton shirtings and prints which are washable are ideal, but silks, fine wools and velvets can also be used, although silks tend to mark where the pins and tacking threads have been. Different fabrics can be used together if they are all of the same weight. Synthetic fabrics are not so successful, as they do not fold easily because of their crease-resistant quality.

Templates can be bought in most needlework shops or cut from cardboard, aluminium or zinc, but it is essential that they are geometrically accurate. If not, the patches will not fit properly together. The shapes most commonly used are hexagons, diamonds, squares and triangles, but many combinations of shapes can be used. *Log-cabin* patchworks are worked in square blocks composed half of light strips and half of dark, stitched and folded around a central square. *Cathedral-window* patchwork is made by folding squares of plain cotton over smaller squares of contrasting coloured fabric.

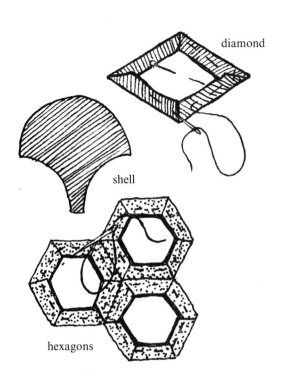

diamond

shell

hexagons

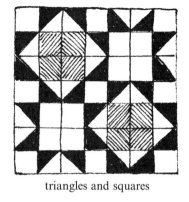

triangles and squares

triangles and squares

boxes

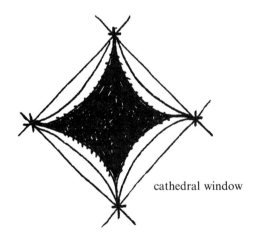

cathedral window

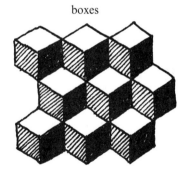

diamond star

log cabin

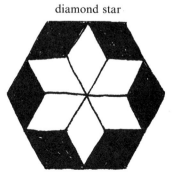

This makes a patchwork of rows of framed diamonds. *Crazy patchwork* is the original patchwork, which can be of scraps of any size arranged on a foundation of cotton. The edges of the patches can be folded under and stitched down through the backing, left and covered with embroidery stitches, or machined down.

The altar frontal for Tetbury church (see page 56) is a good example of a patchwork project in which a range of tones, from dark to light in one colour, read well at a distance and complement the existing furnishings.

Quilting

There are several types of quilting. Plain wadded or English quilting consists of two layers of fabric with a middle layer of wadding. Cord or Italian quilting consists of two layers of fabrics, the design outlined by two narrow lines of stitching, through which a cord is threaded to raise the design. Trapunto also consists of two layers of fabric, with the design stitched in outline and then raised by stuffing the wadding through a small slit inserted in the back, which is afterwards sewn up.

Frames for quilts

In order for the fabric to be under constant tension for quilting, it must be held in a frame. Quilts are quite large, and most of us have little space to have a large frame taking up room for a long period of time; so it is a good idea to have a number of people getting together to work on a quilt to speed up the process. The frame can be constructed from four planks of the length required, clamped together at the corners. Webbing, upon which the backing fabric will be attached, is nailed to the two side planks, known as the runners. The frame can be supported by trestles or on the backs of chairs. Smaller pieces can be worked on an embroidery frame.

Stitch the side edges of the quilt backing to the webbing on the runners, then put on the wadding and finally the top fabric. Smooth flat and pin, starting from the centre outwards. The other ends can be attached by tape pinned through the three layers of fabric, then looped around the frame to keep taut.

The design can be drawn on with tailor's chalk, which easily brushes off. Each stitch must go through all three layers of material, and so must be made in two movements, downwards and then upwards, not in one movement.

Appliqué

Appliqué has been used in several of the quilt projects illustrated. After the motifs have been applied, they can be further embellished with stitchery such as French knots, herringbone stitch or feather stitch. Make sure the grain of the applied motifs corresponds with that of the ground fabric, otherwise it will not lie flat. Thin

fabrics can be ironed on to vilene, which will give body and prevent fraying. Most fabrics lend themselves to appliqué.

Salisbury Cathedral spire-appeal quilt

The Mid Wessex branch of the Embroiderers' Guild wanted to contribute to the Salisbury Cathedral Spire Fund, and I was approached to make designs for a quilt to be raffled. As a number of patchwork quilts had already been made, I wanted to create something a little different and special. I chose magnolia flowers to surround the centre squares of butterflies, dragonflies and bees.

The quilt was to be made from 30 cm (12 in.) squares of cotton lawn upon which I stencilled the flowers, bees and butterflies using a special type of masking film, which can be obtained at good art suppliers. When the backing is peeled off it is slightly tacky on one side, and sticks to the fabric, masking the areas not to be painted.

First the dressing had to be washed out of the fabric, and then the squares were cut out. I covered the table with a plastic cloth, and taped down the fabric squares so that they did not move when positioning and removing the stencil. I used Rowneys screen and fabric printing colour for stencilling, but masking film is excellent for covering areas when spraying with an air brush or spray diffuser.

It is important when stencilling to mix enough of a colour so that you do not run out if doing a particular motif several times; it is difficult exactly to match the same colour again. Use the colour sparingly on the stencil brush, and make a pouncing or jabbing movement to give a good crisp finish. Too much colour on the brush will seep under the stencil. Colours can very effectively be faded into each other, but if applying several colours, use different brushes for each colour.

For the magnolia squares I used a separate stencil mask for each of the four colours, overprinting in some areas. The order in which the colours are printed can make a subtle difference and change the effect. The squares had to be hung up to dry – a clothes-horse or rack is ideal; they were then ironed to make the colour permanent.

The squares, with the wadding and the muslin backing, were placed in plastic bags complete with instructions, to be given out to be quilted by individual workers. When all the squares had been quilted, another group skilfully joined them together and lined the quilt.

The Marchwood Women's Institute quilt

This quilt was made by 20 members of the Marchwood branch of the Women's Institute as part of a Federation quilt project. Yvonne Hayward co-ordinated the project, chose the fabrics and made up the quilt. The borders are

72 The Marchwood Women's Institute quilt: a machine-made sampler quilt.

navy blue, making a good contrast with the lighter, patterned patchwork squares. Each of the squares demonstrates a different set and combination of shapes; the house represents the homecraft aspect of the Women's Institute.

This is a true sampler quilt, machine-made and washable. It was chosen to represent Hampshire in the Federation project, and was exhibited in London along with quilts from other branches.

The Isle of Wight quilt

The Isle of Wight quilt was organized by Barbara Middlebrook and worked by members of the Isle of Wight Embroiderers' Guild, taking two years to complete. It depicts 14 of the island's well-known landmarks, and these are worked in a variety of techniques, to give both the novice and the skilled embroiderer the opportunity to share in the project.

The central panel depicts the Isle of Wight county coat of arms in gold and silver. The predominant colours are blues, browns, golds, and ochres, the borders being in dark navy-blue. The quilted bands of traditional English quilting depict land, sea and air transport, on which the island relies. I think the quilt makes a very appealing advertisement to encourage holiday visitors to come to the island. It is to be displayed at Carisbrooke Castle.

'Texture of Fabric – Texture of Life'

'Texture of Fabric – Texture of Life' is a co-operatively made quilted wall-hanging produced in an arts workshop at the California Institution for Women, a state prison. The workshop began in October 1982 and continued until June 1983. The project, led by artists Susan Hill and Terry Blecher, was part of a continuous programme of arts in social institutions sponsored by Los Angeles Theatre Works. Funding for the project came primarily from the California Arts Council and the California Department of Corrections.

The wall-hanging consists of three panels with embroidered fabric blocks appliquéd on an intricately quilted grey background. The two outer panels, each 183 × 91 cm (6 × 3 ft) show symbols of the outside world and of prison. The 'Neighborhood Panel' contains images of

home. The traditional 'schoolhouse' appliqué design was presented as a starting point. Typically for the workshop, the idea was adopted and modified by the members, and the results range from an adobe under palm trees to a delicate and complex three-storey nineteenth-century house surrounded by rose bushes. Included in this panel are three remarkable squares by the children of a class member, worked while the children (aged six, eight and 12 years) visited their mother in prison. These blocks, presented side by side as the central band of the panel, show the house where the children now live. The band is underscored by a phrase from the mother's writing 'Children's hope of Mother coming home . . .', and the band is placed opposite an image of the mother's cell on the corresponding 'Prison Panel'. The background for the 'Neighborhood Panel' is a colourfully quilted street map, drawn from memory because maps are not allowed in prison.

The 'Prison Panel' is the most sombre in tone, and contains the darkest colours. This panel depicts the harsh reality of prison, with images of barred windows, a corridor of locked doors and heavy keys. An image of brilliantly coloured women slipping through an hourglass is included in this panel. Even in the most serious theme, the humour of the women is evident, particularly in one block, a sculptured representation of prison food. Black watchtowers with giant red eyes are placed at the outermost corners of this panel. The quilting pattern is interlocked bars.

The main panel is 183 × 183 cm (6 × 6 ft), twice the size of the side panels. Radiating from the centre are embroidered images, symbols of the women's most cherished dreams and aspirations. The centre is a pinwheel formed over a pieced ground; this supports the portraits of five racially different women. This image was designed by the women very early on as the emblem for the workshop. Surrounding the centre in a strong diamond configuration are blocks, both individually and co-operatively drawn and embroidered. The 'Neighborhood' and 'Prison' panels are arranged in similar diamonds which intersect the central diamond, linking all three panels. The images of the main panel include embroidered sketches of class members, scenes of mothers with children,

73 The Isle of Wight quilt (1985), organized by Barbara Middlebrook and made by Isle of Wight Embroiderers' Guild. Fourteen of the island's landmarks are depicted in a variety of techniques. (*The Embroiderers' Guild*)

74 The 'Texture of Life' quilt, made at the California Institution for Women (1982/3). (*Judith Pacht*)

fantasy environments, and representations of important memories – for one her truck, for another her Oregon cabin and view of the mountains. These images, placed over a chain-link patterned background, are circled by an enormous ring of hands, which also reach into the 'Neighborhood' and the 'Prison' panels.

In discussions about prison life, the women acknowledged both the commonly understood negative qualities of life in prison, and positive aspects rarely articulated. All felt very protective about the real friendships they had developed, and about the various ways in which each maintained her humanity in a life of severe deprivation and regulation. The ring of hands indicates this connection, protection and struggle. The hands, worked in primary colours, are drawn from life and perform various gestures. Stencilled on the hands are phrases from the women's writings which describe life in prison.

The workshop participants have numbered over 150 women from inside and outside the prison. Susan Hill and Terry Blecher are the workshop directors and originators of the project with Los Angeles Theatre Works. Susan Hill was head of needlework for Judy Chicago's 'The Dinner Party', and Terry Blecher was a principal textile artist on that project. These women were assisted by L.A. Hassing, an expert needleworker, and others who had worked on 'The Dinner Party'. Other 'outside' women included Los Angeles Theatre Works staff and various friends. In the 'inside' group of participants, as with any group, a small number worked consistently, conceptualizing the design and producing work, while a great many participated for a short time. Each participant, whether 'inside' or 'outside', was accorded a full and equal voice in the project. Decisions were reached by argument, persuasion and then a vote.

The Goodworth Clatford quilt

The following description was supplied by Mrs Alwyn Tucker.

'This project was undertaken as a memento of the Goodworth Clatford Women's Institute diamond jubilee, and was commenced in 1983 and completed in 1984; 22 members took part.

'At the concept stage a group of interested ladies met to discuss practicalities, and it was decided that an "all-stitched wall-hanging" should be made, with no glue, paper or card; it would not be framed or have a glass covering, as it was felt that there might be insurance problems, and also much of the effect would be lost. It was then decided that the hanging should

75 The Goodworth Clatford Women's Institute quilt (1983/4). (*Clatford Women's Institute*)

feature a selection of panels depicting the most well-known scenes of the village as they were at the time.

'The three top panels would show the three main buildings of the village, these being the church, the village club and the school. The panels each side of the centrepiece would be the most well-known village views, and the bottom three panels would show an old village house, the recreation ground (for the children), and the new complex of housing finished in 1983. A central panel depicting the Hampshire rose with suitable wording would, we hoped, tie the picture together, and the borders would be quilted with many and various rural scenes of fish, flowers and birds.

'At this time none of the participants had ever attempted anything of this nature before, but we felt that by taking each problem as it arose, we would be able to cope. At the end of the first meeting each person took home a large piece of computer paper, to draw, in their own way and to their own capability, the scene or view of their choice.

'At the next meeting time was spent discussing fabrics, and how the pieces would be fastened to the backing. The simplest way, it seemed, was to have pieces of fabric the colour of the sky on which to attach everything. These in turn would be sewn on to a large backcloth as completed pictures. Many ideas began to develop at this time; seasons, shadows, and textures were discussed, also colours, which could be very deceptive.

'Apart from collecting suitable bits of fabric and purchasing the sky material, not a great deal more was done until January 1984 when we started a regular Monday afternoon session, with anything between two and eight ladies attending. To begin with, each lady took a picture and traced each shape or feature on to greaseproof paper, to make patterns. They they selected fabrics they thought were suitable, cut out the patterns, and pinned them to the sky background. At this point the pictures were passed round so that everyone could comment on the choice of material, and after agreement the tacking began. This was quite fiddly and some coped better than others – all the pictures looked pretty ragged at this stage. The next thing was the machining, and each tiny piece was first of all stay-stitched (just run round);

then, with my new Bernina switched to satin stitch, I began to fix each piece down properly, changing cottons for each colour. It was amazing what a difference it made to have no rough edges, and we were all very encouraged at the effect.

'A particularly gifted girl, Anne Sellars, made the Hampshire rose and all the letterings, and also marked out the background fabric, which was chosen as a neutral shade to tone with the pictures, and also the village club, where the quilt was to be displayed, and once this was done everything began to fall into place. A couple of clever embroiderers 'helped' one or two of the pictures, by adding flowers, leaves, and a little texture here and there. It really made such a difference.

'The next thing to decide on was the quilting motif around the borders, and eventually we settled on the rather attractive "burdock" spray, as this plant grows by the river. The name Clatford means "the ford where the burdock grows" so it couldn't have been more appropriate.

'Now our wall-hanging/collage/quilt was developing and had to be put together, so we borrowed a quilting frame from Ann Ohlenschlager (a good friend and adviser) and "got tacking". We had just a fortnight to go, with 18 sprays of burdock to be quilted, all before the panels could be attached to the backing. Many of the ladies had never quilted before, but with a quick lesson on some spare fabric, they were let loose!

'We were almost there, but it was obvious that for full effect the pictures themselves had also to be quilted. It was not an easy task, quilting through all those layers, but we did our best in the time we had. A curtain pole was kindly donated by a member, and I made hanging straps to suspend the quilt from; at last we were finished.

'Although in total it had taken over a year to make, if we had stuck to it I am sure we could have done it in half the time. The most difficult thing seems to be to get the people together, and to get them to complete their "bit". Now that it is finished, I think it was really worthwhile.

'Now our quilt is hanging in the village club for all to see. It measures 168 × 137 cm (5 ft 6 in. × 4 ft 6 in.), and always stimulates some comment about the village. We feel that it is our

76 A quilt made by the Romsey Quilters' Guild. A quilted map of the town is surrounded by patchwork motifs.

little bit of history, and are very proud of our achievement as a group.'

The Romsey quilt

This quilt was made and financed by about 30 members of the Romsey Quilters' Guild to hang in the town hall. Joyce Downer organized the arrangement of the quilt, which depicts in the centre a quilted map of the town, surrounded by historical buildings and patchwork motifs on a navy-blue ground.

The quilt was mounted on a frame consisting of four 305×13 cm (10 ft $\times$ 5 in.) softwood planks, held at the corners by G-clamps; this made an easily portable frame which can be quickly assembled. Strips of 8 cm (3 in.) wide denim were folded double and stapled on to the planks, and the quilt was pinned to these with long quilters' pins.

12
Work by children

The South Birmingham Young Embroiderers' Society group panel

This panel, measuring 106 × 46 cm (42 × 18 in.), was worked by a dedicated group of young embroiderers aged between eight and 17. They meet regularly once a month for two hours at the Birmingham Museum and Art Gallery. The classes originated from a two-day workshop organized by the Embroiderers' Guild, the results of which delighted the adult helpers.

The theme chosen for the panel was high-rise environment, which is seen every day by the children living in the city. Each young embroiderer was given a piece of light ferracolta fabric: binca for the younger children at six holes per 2.5 cm (1 in.) to use on the high-rise buildings, and bincarette for the older girls with ten holes

per 2.5 cm (1 in.); the overall size of each piece was approximately 28 × 20 cm (11 × 8 in.) In order to produce a wide variation in the finished work, the children were given a vast number of books to look at, dealing with house and building shapes and stitches, but each embroiderer was left to introduce her own ideas. All the embroidery was carried out in white thread, but the children could choose from perlé, stranded cotton, coton-à-broder, or a mixture of all three.

After each of the 18 pieces had been embroidered a cardboard shape was cut to the size of the building, and using PVA adhesive the embroidery was secured to the card by gluing the turnings on to the back of the shaped card. Some of the younger children found this quite difficult, and help was given as necessary.

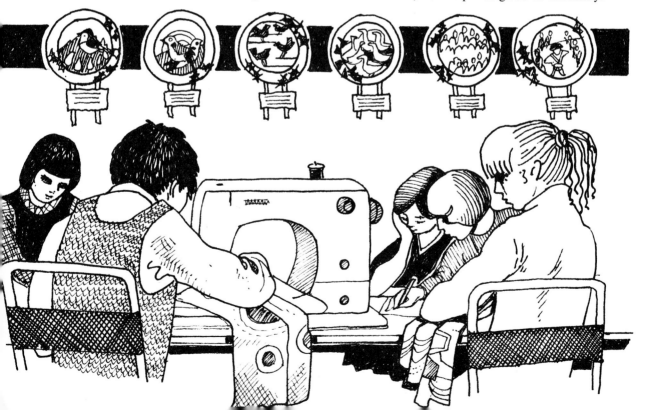

77 The Birmingham Young Embroiderers' Society panel – 106 × 46 cm (42 × 18 in.). The quilt was worked by young embroiderers, aged eight to 17, on the theme of the high-rise environment.

For the background a piece of 6 mm ($\frac{1}{4}$ in.) plywood was used, which had been covered in natural hessian and glued on the reverse side with PVA; the edges of the board were first covered with masking tape. Upon this the embroidered shapes, with the exception of one or two which were laid direct to the background, were then arranged, some overlapping, to obtain the desired effect. Each building was then glued and tacked in place with upholstery tacks; the result was a true skyline effect. To finish the panel, a piece of calico was sewn over the back, and screw-eyes attached for hanging.

Mary Roberts was responsible for the completion of the panel, and for the past two years she has been the mainstay of the group. The panel was exhibited at the Midland Ideal Home Exhibition on the Embroiderers' Guild stand, and at the 1984 Clarendon House exhibition, near Salisbury.

The Syderstone School project

This wall-hanging was made under the guidance of Mrs Shelagh Dashfield who teaches at Syderstone, Norfolk, a small village school with only 42 children and two teachers.

The panels were drawn entirely by the children, 14 girls between five and 11 years old, using fabric-dye crayons and pens on calico. The hanging was then quilted in English and trapunto. Mrs Dashfield explained: 'We did our own version of trapunto. Instead of inserting the filling in the usual way, we teased our filling to the shape needed, and then quilted round it. It had to be simple but effective.' The panel took six weeks to complete; the children worked on it every Friday afternoon, and during wet playtimes. The theme was Syderstone village, and the children produced some very lively pictures, including their school in the centre, the church, pub, shop, mushroom farm, cottages and gardens, flowers in a cottage window, bees and hives, butterflies, a field of rape, and the common with its rare Natterjack toads. The lettering was done in chain stitch. The hanging measures 278 × 165 cm (9 ft 2 in. × 5 ft 5 in.), and was finally put together with a bright red border by Mrs Dashfield.

Cranborne Middle School

Cranborne Middle School, Hampshire, is very fortunate in having Miss Bartlett to inspire the pupils to work together on imaginative projects. Although she is severely handicapped and is unable to do any hand sewing, she can operate a Viking sewing machine which has been adapted to her special requirements. One of her main

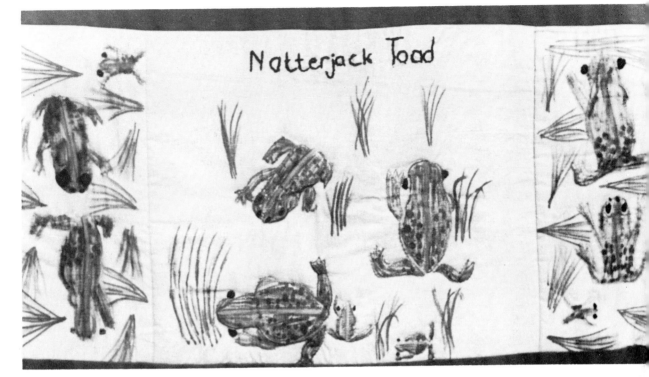

78 The Syderstone hanging, made by children aged five to eleven. The design was drawn on calico and then quilted. (*Shelagh Dashfield*)

79 A detail from the Syderstone hanging. (*Shelagh Dashfield*)

aims is to teach her pupils to become familiar with their sewing machines, using zigzag and free stitching to attach and embellish small pieces of fabric which are put together to make up large hangings.

The designs are first worked up in the art department. Miss Bartlett favours accurate and representational designs which are broken down into sections to be worked by individual pupils. The designs are traced on to vilene, and the small pieces of fabric of many weights and textures are lightly attached using Copydex. Usually I would not advise this, as Copydex tends to come through and stain the surface, but for children who want to get on and finish their work quickly, it is a way of speeding things up and saves pinning and tacking. The fabrics are then stitched down by machine.

This is an excellent way to teach children to use the sewing machine with confidence. Many people I know treat their machine with awe, never mastering the monster or getting the best

from it, so it is a great advantage to give children the opportunity to practise machining, where control is all important.

One of the large hangings, which graces the corridor near the school's entrance, commemorates the 'Millennium', and depicts the important buildings of the area. The buildings or trees were all worked by individual children, and Miss Bartlett had the task of assembling them on the background fabric and stitching them down with zigzag stitch. This hanging took one year and involved all the children in the school. The crafts festival banner, which was exhibited and admired at the Clarendon exhibition in 1984, took only two months, between 40 and 50 third-year children taking part in its creation.

The Christmas carol 'The Twelve Days of Christmas' was chosen as a theme to decorate twelve 30 cm (12 in.) round plaques to be used as Christmas decorations. These are very successful, and can be brought out looking fresh each Christmas. It is a charming project for a school.

111

80 The Cranborne Middle School hanging, showing various local buildings worked in machine embroidery.

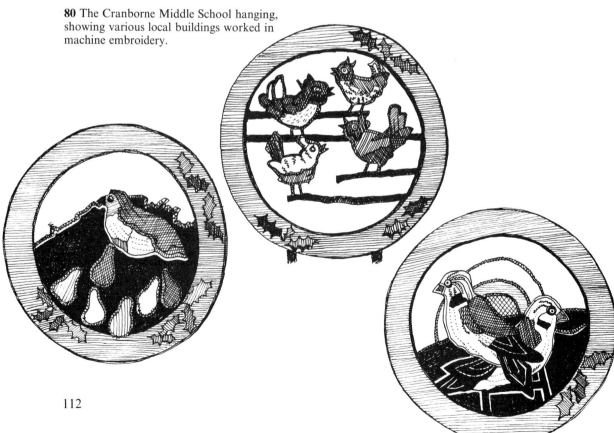

The Crestwood School hangings, Eastleigh, Hampshire

Crestwood School has a very unusual and modern design. Between the two main buildings is a long, high, curved glass-covered area, which has thirty 9 m (30 ft) trees growing from the paving, small coffee tables with multi-coloured umbrellas, and brilliant yellow-painted staircases; it makes a focal point for the children to meet, and to sit and eat their snacks.

On the high brick walls hang four large panels depicting the four seasons. They hang in pairs, and the bright clear colours are very striking. In proportions and style they contribute very successfully to the architecture. The children, aged 12 to 13 years, used torn-paper techniques to prepare designs for the project. Their many and varied ideas were pooled, and with the help of their art teacher and students from the Winchester School of Art, the best features of the children's work were assembled to form the final four designs.

The design was photographed, and then projected on to the fabric to be marked out. The fabric was rip-stock nylon, which is used in the making of hot-air balloons. This is very colourfast and so far has not faded at all; also, it seems not to fray. This is a very successful method for creating large panels, and a relatively quick way of achieving a spontaneous and happy atmosphere in a large area. (See colour plate 11.)

13
Organizations

The Royal School of Needlework

25 Princes Gate, London SW7 1QE. Tel: 01 589 0077/584 4893

The Royal School of Needlework was founded in 1872 by Her Royal Highness Princess Christian, daughter of Queen Victoria, with the aim of restoring ornamental needlework to the high place it once held among the decorative arts.

The high quality of needlework produced by the staff is unsurpassed, and today the school's most important roles are those of teaching and restoration work. Classes are held for both skilled and amateur embroiderers, and under an apprenticeship scheme students learn all forms of needlework techniques. There are at present ten girls apprenticed under the Manpower Services Commission scheme.

In the past, many outstanding commissions have been undertaken in the school's workrooms, including the coronation robes worn by Queen Elizabeth the Queen Mother in 1937, and by Queen Elizabeth at her coronation in 1953.

The Embroiderers' Guild

Apartment 41a, Hampton Court Palace, East Molesey, Surrey KT8 9AU. Tel: 01 943 1229

The Embroiderers' Guild promotes the craft of embroidery at its Hampton Court headquarters, where members may attend classes and workshops on all aspects of embroidery. In addition, it owns a unique study-collection of historical and twentieth-century embroidery and an invaluable reference library of specialist books for members' use. There are over 120 affiliated branches throughout Great Britain, meeting regularly for classes, workshops and other activities.

The Young Embroiderers' Society

The Young Embroiderers' Society was started in 1974 by Lynette de Denne, after a very successful exhibition of children's work in London. Its aims are to encourage the embroiderers of the future. Workshops are regularly held at the Embroiderers' Guild headquarters at Hampton Court, and three newsletters a year are sent out containing ideas for fabric and thread, as well as competitions, quizzes, and news.

The society is open to boys and girls between the ages of five and 18, and membership forms are available from the Embroiderers' Guild, Hampton Court Palace.

The Conservation Centre

Apartment 22, Hampton Court Palace, East Molesey, Surrey KT8 9AU. Tel: 01 977 4943

In 1959 a conservation studio was started by Karen Finch in her own home, and in 1975 the Conservation Centre was opened at Hampton Court. It does invaluable work for museums, the National Trust, and for other public and private bodies.

Karen Finch has an international reputation and has worked tirelessly in the once much-neglected field of conservation. Textiles are particularly vulnerable to wear and tear, and also to pollution in the atmosphere. A course in textile conservation is run for students at Hampton Court.

If you have a textile in need of repair or conservation, seek the advice of the Conservation Centre before attempting anything. The centre will wash and dry-clean precious textiles. Karen Finch does not recommend the spraying of fabrics with commercial fabric-protector.

The '62 Group and the Practical Study Group

Both these groups are affiliated to the Embroiderers' Guild.

The '62 Group was established in 1962. Its aims are to bring professionalism into the creative side of embroidery, to exhibit new work rather than established embroidery, and to improve the standards in schools.

The aim of the Practical Study Group is to further interest in design and embroidery through adult teaching in any part of the country other than London. To join, candidates have to show work for selection, and after five years are re-assessed for continued membership.

Suppliers

Ells & Farrier
5 Princes Street
Hanover Square
London W1
Imitation stones, beads, sequins

The Embroidery Shop
51 William Street
Edinburgh EH3 7LW
DMC threads, linens, Appleton wools, canvas,
books, etc. Mail-order enquiries welcome

Frisk Products Ltd
Unit 4
Franthorne Way
Bellingham Trading Estate
London SE6
Masking film for stencilling

Michael Hand
25 Lexington Street
Golden Square
London W1
Military cords

Irish Linen Depot
39 Bond Street
Ealing
London W5 5AS
Pure linen, scrim, etc.

Latex Cushion Company
830 Kingsbury Road
Erdington
Birmingham B24 9PU
Latex for making up kneelers

John Lewis
Oxford Street
London W1
Fabrics and haberdashery

Liberty & Co. Ltd
Regent Street
London W1
Thai and Indian silks, fabrics

Mace and Nairn
89 Crane Street
Salisbury
Wiltshire SP1 2PY
Embroidery threads and equipment

McCulloch & Wallis Ltd
25/6 Dering Street
London W1R 0BU
Haberdashery, vilenes, Bondaweb, Bondina,
polyester boning

The Patchwork Dog and Calico Cat
21 Chalk Farm Road
London NW1
Patchwork and quilting supply shop

The Royal School of Needlework
25 Princes Gate
London SW7
Metal threads, gold and silver cords, canvas,
wools, etc.

Silken Strands
33 Links Way
Gatley
Cheadle
Cheshire SK8
Machine embroidery threads, beads, leather,
snake-skins, shisha mirrors. Mail order only.
For brochure send stamp

Wilton Royal Carpet Factory Ltd
King Street
Wilton
Wiltshire
Carpet thrums

J. Wippell & Co. Ltd:
11 Tufton Street, London SW1
55/6 High Street, Exeter
24/6 King Street, Manchester
Ecclesiastical suppliers

Bibliography

Dean, Beryl, *Ideas for Church Embroidery*, Batsford, 1968

Dean, Beryl, *Embroidery in Religion and Ceremonial*, Batsford, 1981, 1986

Edwards, Joan, *Church Kneelers*, Batsford, 1967

Edwards, Joan, *Crewel Embroidery in England*, Batsford, 1975

Howard, Constance, *Twentieth Century Embroidery in Great Britain 1940–1963*, Batsford, 1982

Howard, Constance, *Twentieth Century Embroidery in Great Britain 1964–1977*, Batsford, 1984

Howard, Constance, *Twentieth Century Embroidery in Great Britain from 1978*, Batsford, 1986

Rhodes, Mary, *Dictionary of Canvas Work Stitches*, Batsford, 1980

Russell, Pat, *Lettering for Embroidery*, Batsford 1971, new edition, 1985

Springall, Diana, *Canvas Embroidery*, Batsford, 1980

Index